D0283345

Our Voices

ISSUES FACING
BLACK WOMEN
IN AMERICA

Our Voices

RACISM, SEXUALITY,

MARRIAGE, SINGLENESS,

SINGLE PARENTING,

THE CHURCH, FINANCES,

SPIRITUALITY, HEALTH,

AND SELF-ESTEEM

amanda johnson,
general editor

MOODY PUBLISHERS
CHICAGO

© 2009 by
AMANDA JOHNSON

All rights reserved. No part of this book may be reproduced in any form without permission in writing from the publisher, except in the case of brief quotations embodied in critical articles or reviews.

Scripture quotations, unless otherwise indicated, are taken from the *Holy Bible, New International Version* ®. NIV®. Copyright © 1973, 1978, 1984 by International Bible Society. Used by permission of Zondervan. All rights reserved.

Scripture quotations marked KJV are taken from the King James Version.

All websites and phone numbers listed herein are accurate at the time of publication but may change in the future or cease to exist. The listing of website references and resources does not imply publisher endorsement of the site's entire contents. Groups and organizations are listed for informational purposes, and listing does not imply publisher endorsement of their activities.

Editor: Kathryn Hall
Interior Design: Ragont Design
Cover Design: LeVan Fisher Design
Cover Photos and Imagery: © Mel Curtis/Getty Images, © Phillip Graybill/
Corbis, and © Vectorstock/Shutterstock Images

Library of Congress Cataloging-in-Publication Data

Our voices : issues facing Black women in America / Amanda Johnson, general editor.
    p. cm.
Includes bibliographical references.
ISBN 978-0-8024-7847-4
1. African American women—Religious life. I. Johnson, Amanda.
BR563.N4O89 2009
277.3'083082—dc22

2009018945

1 3 5 7 9 10 8 6 4 2

Printed in the United States of America

████████████

For Danaeya, Serena, Allyson, Arielle, and Mariah.
The women whose voices matter to me the most.
May each of you be assured that I always want to
hear what's in your heart.

For my parents, Horace Christopher and Alyce Christopher Ballard,
who never let me forget that my voice was worthy to be heard and
showed me what it meant to live with dignity and a sense of purpose.

CONTENTS

Introduction   9

Chapter One
The Spirit-Empowered Life: Jesus Christ, Our Anchor
Yolanda L. Powell   12

Chapter Two
She Shall Be Called Woman: Embracing Who God Says I Am
Sabrina D. Black   36

Chapter Three
Our Purpose: A First Lady's Revolutionary Conversion
Karen Waddles   54

Chapter Four
In Pursuit of a Healthy Lifestyle
Dr. Taffy Anderson   72

Chapter Five
Racial Reconciliation: Our Ministry to Bridge the Gap
Felicia Middlebrooks   90

Chapter Six
Money and Financial Fitness: Stretch, Save, and Share
Lisa A. Crayton   112

Chapter Seven
Sexuality and the Seasons of Life
Amanda Johnson   130

Chapter Eight
The Sojourn of Singles: Decision at the Crossroad
Valerie Clayton   144

Chapter Nine
For Lovers Only: The Sanctity of the Marriage Covenant
Dr. Doretha O'Quinn   160

Chapter Ten
A Single Mother's Assignment: Raising Boys to Be Godly Men
Victoria Saunders Johnson   176

Chapter Eleven
A Single Mother's Assignment: Raising Godly Daughters
Amanda Johnson   198

Biographies of Contributing Writers   222

Acknowledgments   229

INTRODUCTION

Wow! I am impressed, That's what I thought as I placed the handset back on the phone charger. The writers you will hear from in this compilation had just finished a conference call about the scope and purpose of *Our Voices, Issues Facing Black Women in America.* I have no doubt that, as you peruse these pages, you will be as encouraged as I was. Throughout the conversation, the love for our sisters resonated over and again. There was unanimous resolve that this project would effectively inform, inspire, and ignite a desire in the reader to be a dedicated servant in the body of Christ. The enthusiasm of the entire group of writers was infectious and energizing.

Moreover, the eleven chapters in this book were written by ten women from nine states. We come from an array of backgrounds, talents, and careers. Included are a physician, an educator, a university administrator, a radio personality, a financial planner, professional writers, Christian counselors, and single moms. Although we each serve in varied aspects of ministry, we are united in our love of Jesus Christ. Subsequently, all of us love you and we are dedicated to entrusting you with the things we have learned so that you will in turn teach others (2 Timothy 2:2).

The contemporary response to societal challenges, in general, is to allow problems to percolate and escalate to the point of crises of epic proportion. A typical reaction is usually to follow up with the trademark response, which is to "put out fires." However, as women of God, we have monumental challenges that will allow us phenomenal opportunities to have an impact on our families, communities, and society with God-sized solutions to present-day issues.

Throughout the course of human history, God has been about the business of using ordinary people to solve generations of overwhelming challenges: famine (Joseph), natural disaster (Noah), war (David, Gideon), and human suffering (Esther, Moses). These people availed themselves to God to release folks from a plethora of perils, crises, and tight spots. We too can be the answer for our generation because we know the One who has the solutions!

With a scriptural basis, the articulated themes in this collection of articles are as distinctive as the women who wrote them. Chapter 1 on spirituality emphasizes submitting to the will of God, with a special emphasis on the sustaining power of praise and worship in the life of the believer.

To improve the care and nurturing of children, the first objective must be to engage, educate, and empower the adults in their lives. It is a major task for a single parent to make decisions and provide social, emotional, and economic support for their children. Therefore, chapters 10 and 11 address the unique experience of parenting children as single mothers. One is written from the perspective of raising sons; the other serves to encourage mothers of daughters. After all is said and done, home is where life makes up its mind!

An important reminder for weary parents is the reality that there are seasons of life. Fortunately, the parenting phase doesn't last a lifetime. If parents can be engaged, empowered, and encouraged to make the necessary investment while their children are young, they can anticipate the rewards and freedoms of their next season while watching their children succeed in adulthood. Prayerfully, the chapters on parenting will move moms from the knowledge that parenting *should be* a priority to the conviction that parenting *is* the priority.

Chapter 6 on finances discusses the current economic climate of financial downturn, blight, and bailouts. It places a new emphasis on what our attitude should be in regard to money. This chapter offers some very practical advice and strategies that can truly empower us to bolster our personal, family, and collective coffers as part of the Christian community.

There is a healthy discussion in chapter 8 for singles. It covers how they should view their journey and conduct themselves on the road to finding a mate. Moreover, chapter 9 pertains to the marriage covenant and is for women who take their role as Christian wives seriously. It provides a biblical strategy for keeping a marriage union alive and well.

Racial reconciliation and racism are the topic of chapter 5. Politics aside, it has been an amazing thing to see our country elect its first African American president. Yet, there are alarming statistics that trouble the Black population. Black men had an incarceration rate of 3,042 per 100,000 Black men in the United States with Black males ages 30–34 incarcerated at the highest rate overall.[1] Sadly, 35 percent of all African American children live in poverty.[2] Moreover, unemployment is rampant in our cities and there are nutritional food deficiencies in urban areas where you can find fast foods galore but fresh fruits and vegetables are scarce. Many of these disparities are direct or indirect consequences of racism.

Chapter 3 is a discussion on the role of women in the local church. It focuses on the tremendous opportunities for women to minister and encourage each other as discipleship helpers and mentors.

To round off our aim to address the many pertinent issues facing Black women, another topic deals with sexuality (chapter 7), in light of the various seasons of life women find themselves in. There is also discourse about the issues of self-concept (chapter 2) and the impact of obesity on health (chapter 4).

It has been the goal of Moody Publishers to give a significant voice to African American Evangelical Christians who have been effectively disenfranchised and marginalized by the established media. I am grateful to them for the Lift Every Voice division. However, a voice is only significant if there are those who are willing to hear. Thank you for the opportunity to share our perspectives based on the Word of God with you. May you be edified and motivated to further study and personal application.

May God strengthen the work of your hands!

—*Amanda*

Chapter One

THE SPIRIT-EMPOWERED LIFE:
JESUS CHRIST, OUR ANCHOR

We have this hope as an anchor
for the soul, firm and secure . . .

—HEBREWS 6:19

Yolanda L. Powell

Black Christian women have traditionally overcome obstacles and troubling circumstances by remaining faithful to the spiritual anchors of our faith that are grounded in Jesus Christ. Our spiritual life is important to our existence; it is the most valuable asset that we possess. The health of our very soul is, indeed, prime in the shifting tides of twenty-first-century life.

I learned this early on as a young girl. Nearly fifty years later, I can still see the visible faith of the elder mothers in my family. They rocked away pain and problems like valiant warriors, prayed by the side of the bed to an invisible God, hummed the songs of Zion with tears of joy, read their old worn Bibles for daily sustenance, and then dressed in their Sunday-go-to-meeting finest, despite the menial jobs they held all week long. I sigh with joy and pride at the remembrance of this and gain new strength each time I reflect upon it. These women were obviously anchored in a Holy God. None of life's storms seemed to blow them off course.

What a grand life they led in the Spirit! How rich in faith they were despite the rags of segregation and the working-class stigma of second-class citizenship. What noble and honorable women they were in Christ! These Christian matriarchs made constant sacrifices and vowed to leave for us a legacy of strong faith and eternal hope in Jesus Christ—the Light of Life!

The hums and hugs, worship and wisdom of these women speak volumes! How did they survive and overcome harsh days and bitter nights? In what ways did they stand despite racial prejudice and gender bias? From where did their strength and sustenance come during weak and painful times? How did they thrive? How must we? Truly, they were empowered by the Spirit with an anchor of the soul! If we ignore this spiritual truth, we could possibly thwart our spiritual compass and be driven recklessly off course! For after all, Jesus told us that it is indeed possible to gain the whole world and lose our soul (Matthew 16:26).

Therefore, we must revisit the timeless elements that kept and sustained the lives of our spiritual foremothers; for their "anchors" can be embraced and passed on in a modern age—if we will only believe and receive the help they offer and the spiritual richness that will take place deep inside.

TIMELESS ELEMENTS OF OUR SPIRITUAL ANCHOR

An *anchor* is described as a person or entity. It is that which can be relied on for support, stability, or security; a source that we can depend on for safety. An anchor is a sort of mainstay or an emblem of hope. Every life needs one in tow. Why? Anchors keep us on a straight course and refuse to allow the tempest and gale to alter our direction. What a necessity. There are at least four timeless elements that comprise the proverbial anchor in the lives of Black Christian women. These elements have given us the ability to endure trouble, overcome trials, and persevere through tribulation: 1) Saving faith in Jesus Christ as Redeemer and Deliverer; 2) Uncompromising belief in God's Holy Word; 3) Prayers uttered with an unshakable trust; and 4) Worship and singing aloud songs, hymns, and spiritual songs.

Saving Faith in Jesus Christ as Redeemer and Deliverer

The Incarnate God, Jesus Christ, is the source of eternal life through personal redemption and social deliverance. He is the only One who can right the wrongs of this life, clean up our tarnished record of sin, and bring reconciliation to the instability of our reckless souls. Faith in the Living Lord and in His ability to rectify and restore provides the believing woman with the most powerful tool that she can possess to weather the storms of fear, discouragement, and resignation. The ageless triumph of Christ on the cross and the promise of eternal life in glory with Him is the "blessed hope" that defies all of the negative odds weighed against women of faith.

When God says, *"Keep your lives free . . . and be content with what you have, because God has said, 'Never will I leave you; never will I forsake you'"* (Hebrews 13:5)—He means it! We believe His Word because *"God is not a man, that he should lie, nor a son of man, that he should change his mind. Does he speak and then not act? Does he promise and not fulfill?"* (Numbers 23:19). If God said it, He will do it and the confidence and esteem that this breeds in the believing heart of Black Christian women work wonders in our soul. With all of our sisters in unison, we declare that *"The Lord is my helper; I will not be afraid. What can man do to me?"* (Hebrews 13:6). This assurance grants peace and relieves burdens. It's a "sister-secret" we must promise to keep and share as an anchor of the soul!

Furthermore, faith in the death, burial, and resurrection of Jesus assures us that "trouble won't last always" and that the Lord already has a grand plan to protect, prosper, and perfect our lives. We are certain of the fact that *"weeping may remain for a night, but rejoicing comes in the morning"* (Psalm 30:5). No matter what we're going through with our spouses, children, parents, kinfolks, pastors, supervisors, or co-workers—Jesus will work it out and bring light and illumination to every dark area.

Now, here's the spiritual reality: Things don't always work out the way that we plan, or even with a favorable outcome; but God promises to be *"our refuge and strength, an ever-present help in trouble"* (Psalm 46:1). We must be comforted by this spiritual truth and look for the All-Powerful One to show up—one way or another! In the process of discovering reality and truth—Jesus does work through every situation in our lives to ultimately bring about godly character in us for our ultimate good. Despite it all, however, God is yet for us and He is still good! Jesus, then, is the primary anchor of the soul for the Black Christian woman.

Uncompromising Belief in God's Holy Word

The primary foundation of our lives as women of faith is based on an uncompromising belief in the Holy Scriptures. According to author Michelle White, "The Bible is the collection of sacred texts that attest to the existence of God, catalogues God's victories on behalf of the weak, and gives clear statements of God's loving intentions toward humankind" (White 2002). The relevance and veracity of the Bible make it essential reading for the spiritual well-being of a woman yielded and empowered by the Spirit of God. The Holy Spirit is vital to our walk with Jesus Christ as our Savior and Lord. He was sent to be our "Helper" and "Comforter" and "Guide."

Being led and directed by the Spirit of God is a win-win situation for the believing woman. Even though the way may seem steep or challenging, His presence and power reassures us that we will eventually reach our destination and fulfill our destiny. We become accountable to His leadership and direction and are apt to confess our sins, address toxic habits, and regain daily control of our lives—moment by moment. With this kind of empowerment, we simply will not practice sin or lawlessness and are less prone to carnality and self-deception. As my spiritual sister Kathie often says, "We learn to live truly, deal truly, and love truly! This is the essential undergirding of spiritual empowerment."

Personally, I love the Word of God! It has been a "close companion" to me for over a quarter century. It is chock-full of narrative stories, drama, poetry, history, spiritual insights, and practical instruction to guide our lives. The apostle Peter informs all believers that *"we did not follow cleverly invented stories"* (2 Peter 1:16). In other words, the Scriptures are not a Hollywood script or a fiction novel. They are an account that God Himself delivered to us through different writers and spokesmen at varied times to communicate clearly with us as His children. In every line, He bares His soul and pours out His thoughts.

Peter further exclaims that *"we have the word of the prophets made more certain, and you will do well to pay attention to it, as to a light shining in a dark place, until the day dawns and the morning star rises in your hearts"* (2 Peter 1:19). I agree. The metaphor of the Word being like light is so important for believers to comprehend living in this dark and often confusing world. Let's read to gain spiritual sight and illumination on life issues we do not quite understand.

This is what our ancestors did. The Old Testament resonates with victory and defeat, power and weakness, comfort and despair. Historically, Black slaves listened to stories about Pharaoh and how the children of Israel came to freedom. From these accounts, they made direct comparisons to their internal and external battles with the heartless slave owners. They found comfort as they considered Daniel walking around all night in a den of lions and coming out unharmed. They believed the spoken text and it became a foundation for their faith. They reasoned, if God worked such a miracle for Daniel, would He not do the same for them?

They took hold of Holy Writ and never looked back doubting that the God of Abraham, Isaac, and Jacob is able to deliver. As they listened to the biblical account of the three Hebrew boys who were thrown into the fiery flames and yet were preserved by the presence of Almighty God, they heard the words of Shadrach, Meshach, and Abednego: *"If it be so, our God, whom we serve, is able to deliver us from the burning fiery furnace, and he will deliver us out of thine hand, O king. But if not, be it known unto thee, O king, that we will not serve thy gods, nor worship the golden image which thou hast set up"* (Daniel 3:17–18 KJV).

Now, the good news in all of this is that these patriarchs never boasted in the outcome but in the Lord alone. True faith in God will empower us to prevail and overcome circumstantial hardships regardless of what they may be. As I heard a believing sister say recently, "The truest test of our faith is what we do when we don't come out on top—when things don't work out. When the loved one dies, or we lose our job, or we receive a limited diagnosis." Only the Word of God can give us that kind of spiritual equilibrium. It was so in the time of Daniel, in the days of American slavery, and it can be so for us in a new millennium.

Let's also review the New Testament. The life and times of Jesus, as recorded in the Bible, is quite revolutionary and refreshing—especially in the lives of women. Our Lord showcased our worth and dignity, even when it was quite unpopular to do so. Jesus *alone* brings deliverance from demonic oppression, forgives a sister caught in adultery, and dares the men to cast an inflammatory indictment against her. He heals bleeding bodies, rescues tormented minds, and gives spiritual sight to the blind. He is the Master Defender and Heroic Knight who lifts women to new heights of possibility and acceptance. As Black Christian women, we revel in God's Word because it is a singular place of liberation and a rare domain of empowerment for us.

Author Michelle White describes the Bible poignantly as:

a mirror, [in which] we see ourselves in the person of Naomi, otherwise known as "bitterness" but we also see ourselves in Mary, honored by God.

So much of who we are when we are vulnerable and ill is reflected in the life of Hagar, but in spite of the struggles, Esther and Ruth shine through. We go ahead in Jesus' name because we are more than conquerors. We are as David: adulterous, conniving and yet still beloved of God—a complicated spiritual paradox. We suffer and we triumph, we win more and sometimes we win less. . . . (White 2002)

The Scriptures also pierce and penetrate our person, revealing our true selves like a magnifying lens. They help us to work out our belief systems through transforming the way we think. God's Word is continually correcting and conforming us to the image of Christ. It positions us to be changed and transformed by the renewing of our minds. We come to the conclusion, via the Word, that Almighty God is right and we are wrong. Therefore, we anchor ourselves securely in His Holy Writ and exclaim, "His truth is everlasting and His word endures to all generations!" The Word of God is, indeed, a true anchor of the soul.

Prayers Uttered with an Unshakable Trust

"Prayer is the constant and vital activity of maintaining connection with God who is the source of strength and power," says author Michelle White. It is also a conversation and exchange that fortifies believing women and causes us to *"throw off everything that hinders and the sin that so easily entangles"* so that we can *"run with perseverance the race marked out for us"* (Hebrews 12:1). With all of the "issues of life" from personal and social to emotional and relational, we can cry out, *"lead me to the rock that is higher than I"* (Psalm 61:2) because we know God will hear our prayer.

As Black Christian women, we must learn to cast our enormous cares upon the Lord, knowing He cares for us (1 Peter 5:7). The Father gives us an open invitation to join with Him in a shared relationship of prayer in which we must bring to the time of intimacy a speaking mouth, a listening ear, and an obedient heart. The Lord also makes Himself available and responsible to us in this great exchange and becomes Himself our Chief Intercessor and Wonderful Counselor.

Because of His faithfulness, He hears us deeply, responds to us wisely, and provides us with supernatural comfort and direction. Through this spiritual process of prayer, believing women enter into an intimate relationship with the Holy Spirit. We pray to a caring Father in therapeutic terms that are often a mixture of spoken declarations, mind decrees, heart surrender, unintelligible groans, flowing tears, victorious shouts, and a final exclamation, "In Jesus' name!"

Years ago, through a mixture of trial and error, I learned how to pray simple, passionate prayers that slowly developed into an intimate relationship with our Chief Intercessor, Jesus Christ. Prayer became the central focus of my life and it forged within me a strong reliance upon my Savior. Modeled after the popular "ACTS" of prayer—adoration, confession, thanksgiving, and supplication, here's my personal spin on the acronym for personal development and growth:

A *is for the Acclaim of Precious Adoration.* The first words to part our lips are words of awe, appreciation, and applause. The Lord responds to our sincere and heartfelt words of adoration. Recite the names of God and exalt Him for the different ones that you have experienced over time.

C *is for the Comforting Humility of Confession.* How can we approach God and stand in His presence with unconfessed sin in our hearts? During times of prayer, we seek His mercy and forgiveness. Prayers of confession roll out the proverbial red carpet for the King of Glory to draw near and remove our sins with the cleansing blood of Jesus applied to our hearts.

T *is for the Tremendous Renewal of Thanksgiving.* Knowing that Christ has seen and heard the ugly stuff in my life and still loves me makes me want to worship Him out of the depth of my born-again spirit. This is the aspect of prayer that says, "In spite of all I've done to trample on Your grace, You still cover me with Your wings of mercy. And, I thank You."

S *is for the Sustaining Power of Supplication.* Our hearts fall into deep places of request as we ask God to heal and restore our marriages, convert our children, preserve our jobs, or deliver us from our fears. To supplicate is to entreat and ask earnestly and fervently in prayer. Because God is our everything—Creator, Deliverer, Healer, Savior,

Father, and Friend—there is nothing in us that He cannot change or correct—to please Himself. We must only yield to Him.

Furthermore, over time I have discovered new frontiers in prayer that were stimulating and invigorating. Surrendering to Christ garnered fresh sustenance for my soul and gave me increased power to see changes all around me. Here's a brief list of the prayer empowerment I experienced:

Singing New Songs. Singing helps to remove the "sameness" from spoken words and causes the heart to soar with uncluttered thoughts. It's a fresh, sweet, daily offering to give to the Lord in the midst of telling Him all your troubles. It's a serenade of the spirit that can add a joyful lightness to the time of prayer (Psalms 96:1; 98:1; 144:9; 149:1).

Reciting the Scriptures Aloud. An open Bible is a helpful resource in prayer that greatly empowers your spirit. Praying the Word of God is like having an endless inventory of supply to bombard the heavenlies. Plus, it pleases the Lord to hear His own Word being recited with joy and faith back to Him (Psalm 33:4–9; Isaiah 44:23; 55:11; Romans 10:17).

Incorporating Flexible Movement. Refuse to stay in traditional prayer postures. Walk around the room, swing your arms, clap or lift hands, skip, leap, and jump! I call it exulting over God. There is surely a time to kneel quietly. Yet, be willing to add a time for movement, flexibility, and spontaneity to prayer. It's a sure energy booster and, I believe, a delight to the Lord who made us expressive human beings (Psalms 66; 100).

Lifting My Voice with a Shout. Physical movement often brings verbal explosion. The voice begins to utter aloud joyous words to the King of Glory! This is the time to exalt, magnify, and lift the Father with everything that is within you. Let heaven and hell know that our God rules and reigns forever. Ignite the atmosphere with shouts of His goodness, majesty, dominion, and might (Psalms 47:1–4; 77:1–3; 98:4; Luke 17:15–16)!

Flowing in Intercession for Others. There is so much to pray for: spouses, missionaries, pastors, presidents, neighbors, co-workers, and children. The Holy Spirit wants us to intercede and "stand in the gap" for those we know and love. It's a time when you can be entrusted with the burdens and needs of others and allow the Holy Spirit to lead you to speak on behalf of those who desperately need it (Galatians 4:19; 1 Timothy 2:1; James 5:16–18).

Displaying Deep Emotion without Words. After singing songs and hymns, praying Scripture aloud, and interceding for others, there's another dimension of prayer where words cannot always be uttered. These are the times to weep, laugh, moan, or lament in ways that only God can understand. Such emotions are an important expression of the deepest part of a believing woman. Our heavenly Father is the only One who can read tears (Psalm 130:1–2; Romans 8:26–27; Hebrews 5:7).

Listening to the Father's Closing Remarks. The ultimate joy of prayer is when everything grows still and completely silent in a holy hush. Sometimes strong impressions will arise on the heart or clarity will come with strong illumination to the soul on matters that only the Lord can address. At other times only the sweetness of His presence and goodness speaks and it's clearly understood, although it's not audible. It is important to know that He has the final say, so listen for His acknowledgments and closing remarks (Exodus 19:18–25; 1 Kings 19:12; Psalm 42:1–2).

Prayer is an anchor of the soul and it is time for Black Christian women to find time to spend with the Lord in His personal chamber. Such times will stabilize our hearts and satisfy our souls—and aid us in our spiritual growth and development.

Worship and Singing Aloud Songs, Hymns, and Spiritual Songs

Music has always been a "keeping power" and historic "soul force" for the entire Black community. Even after we came out of the clubs, nightlife, and Soul Train lines, our hearts still resonated with the sounds of music. The rich tones of stereo sound and a need to turn up the radio and sing with childlike joy remained appealing. With their newfound salvation, many new believers were making a shift from R&B to gospel music.

Though the lyrics changed and our Lover was new, the rhythm in life and the syncopated licks of the Spirit never missed a beat. For this we are grateful. How can one have true love like we have found in Jesus Christ and not sing love songs to Him and songs of adoration about Him? Vocal expressions through music have been a mainstay for Black Christian women. *We sing because we're happy! We sing because we're free!*

In fact, music was a main ingredient of our liberation for freedom and equality. It began with the old Negro spirituals, such as, "If God Delivered Daniel, Why Not Us?" or "There Is a Balm in Gilead." According to the website NegroSpirituals.com, some of the earlier spirituals were inspired by African music. Although these tunes were like hymns, many were called "shouts" because they were accompanied with typical dancing, hand clapping, and foot tapping.

In the Black Christian tradition, there was also something called a "call and response chant" in which the preacher (leader) sings one verse and the congregation (chorus) answers the leader with another verse. This type of interaction can be experienced in such songs as "Swing Low Sweet Chariot." The leader says, "Swing low, sweet chariot" and the chorus responds, "Coming for to carry me home." Songs such as these still have the ability to minister to our souls and give us hope for a brighter day.

During the 1960s, in our struggle for civil rights, Negro spirituals like "We Shall Overcome," "Oh Freedom," and "This Little Light of Mine" emerged out of our social dilemmas and were sung with great faith and power. The songs of Zion focused our hearts and regulated our hearts for change. As our community moved from traditional Negro spirituals into newer gospel songs, the lyrics focused on praising the Lord, personal improvement, and the beloved community.

Many of these songs were inspired by social problems like segregation, a lack of brotherly love, and the infiltration of drugs and hopelessness among youth. In the 1970s, many songs like "Oh Happy Day" by Edwin Hawkins created the pop-gospel sound. Instruments were significant in the accompaniment of the singers who were often assembled in choirs. Ministers such as James Cleveland and musicians like Mattie Moss Clark led us into higher forms of praise that still "shake, rock, and roll" the House of God (NegroSpirituals.com).

Our lives are deeply empowered and strongly anchored by music. I can still hear Tramaine Hawkins singing, "I'm Goin' Up Yonder" and "Holy One." Then there's "Amazing Grace" and "Precious Lord" sung by Mahalia Jackson that still bring tears of adoration and deep appreciation to a ransomed and redeemed soul. Within the heart of believing women, there has always been a song of worship and praise that anchors us in the middle of a storm. The Word of God teaches us the importance of relying on music as a spiritual tool:

Do not get drunk on wine, which leads to debauchery. Instead, be filled with the Spirit. Speak to one another with psalms, hymns and spiritual songs. Sing and make music in your heart to the Lord, always giving thanks to God the Father for everything, in the name of our Lord Jesus Christ. (Ephesians 5:18–20)

Music is a mainstay and a power source for the Christian woman of African American descent. We can express our thankfulness to our Lord through enjoying spiritual music. Singing along gives us a joyful heart and keeps us from relying on prescription drugs, alcohol consumption, or other medicating stimulants to merely cope with life. We have learned to soothe our aching souls by listening to the melodious voice of CeCe Winans, the worshipful songs of Israel Houghton, the powerful exhortations of Shirley Caesar, or the ecstatic in-your-face-sounds of Tye Tribbett.

It is obvious that Black Christians, and especially women, literally crooned our way out of mental and physical slavery; waltzed our entire race into acceptable forms of citizenship and civil rights; encouraged our hearts—despite the effects of racism; and undergirded our personal faith through creative hooks and lyrics performed through a musical venue. Singing is an anchor of the African American body, soul, and spirit. It can never be ignored as a timeless and essential element of our faith in Almighty God. *"Shout for joy to the Lord, all the earth. Worship the Lord with gladness; come before him with joyful songs. Know that the Lord is God. It is he who made us, and we are his; we are his people, the sheep of his pasture"* (Psalm 100:1–3).

THE VALUE OF SPIRITUAL SELF-NURTURE

Now that we have been reacquainted with the anchors that can keep our spiritual lives from being tossed and driven, let us examine in greater detail the importance of nurturing our spiritual selves. Neglecting this critical area of our lives affects our internal posture and God-confidence. We'll also review the factors that threaten our spiritual empowerment through pitfalls and stumbling blocks of secular spirituality and inhibit our ability to empower others around us. Finally, we'll offer some practical strategies on how to continually lean on the Lord in modern times and daily surrender to His sovereign will and perfect way.

Nurturing the Image of God Within

> *So God created man in his own image, in the image of God he created him;*
> *male and female he created them.* (Genesis 1:27)

> *When God created man, he made him in the likeness of God. He created them*
> *male and female and blessed them. And when they were created, he called*
> *them 'man'.* (Genesis 5:12, emphasis added)

These passages in Genesis are two of the most powerful verses in all of God's Word, as it relates to women. Without a doubt, we were created in *imago Dei* (God's image) and He designed women according to His spiritual likeness—just like our male counterparts. This forever settles the issue of our spiritual worth and catapults us into spiritual prominence.

"Our first parents entered the universe by cosmic conception marvelously fashioned to reflect God, relate to God, rule under God and rest in God," writes Robert W. Kellerman in *Soul Physicians: A Theology of Soul Care and Spiritual Direction.* "Karl Barth called the *imago Dei* the *Magna Carta* of humanity because it is God's supreme declaration of our design, dignity, and destiny. A proper understanding of the *imago Dei* is crucial for healthy relationships—how we relate to God, others and ourselves" (Kellerman 2005, p 126).

It is important that we have a healthy and robust spirit life, because it is an "image gift" given to us by God Himself that reflects His own Spirit. *"God is spirit, and his worshipers must worship in spirit and in truth"* (John 4:24).

Essentially, nurturing our spiritual selves is born out of a love relationship with the true and living God. The quality of our conforming to the image of Jesus Christ is directly related to the quantity of time that we spend in making ourselves available to experience His transforming power. It took my teenage son, Jordan, to help me understand the importance and simplicity of this truth. "The mind experiences growth through reading and education," he began. "The body gets stronger with exercise and proper nutrition; but the spirit only grows and matures through a personal relationship with God that is characterized by consistent time in His Word and prayer." As women, we must embrace God's love wholeheartedly and take full advantage of all that He affords us in Christ.

In my first book, *Soul Food & Living Water: Spiritual Nourishment and Practical Help for African-American Families* (Powell & Powell 2003), I shared about my spiritual transformation in Christ and how I fell in love with the Master all over again. He taught me how to nurture my soul and to keep my spiritual life ignited for His own good pleasure. Below are seven ways I learned to embrace the living Word and to spend time in the awesome presence of God:

Daily Quiet Time. In light of the importance of Holy Scripture, time must be set aside every day for personal devotion with the Master. Our fore-parents called these special moments "stealing away." It's time that we literally take away from other activities in order to spend time alone with the True Lover of our very souls.

Journal Writing and Note Taking. Enjoy the pleasure of recording prayers, Bible truths, dreams, lessons learned, agonizing defeats, amazing victories, conversations with comrades, wisdom from the elders, and spiritual directives from the Lord Himself. As you open a fresh page, also give the Lord a clean and empty heart so He can fill it with His will and desire.

Personalizing the Psalms and Other Passages. Since God's Word is so relevant and significant in the life of a believer, we should put all of our trust into it as the never fading, never-changing, revealed will of God. Learn to take passages and write them out in ways that summarize or simplify the text and make it easier for you to understand. Enter the process by breaking things down to elementary terms, looking words up in the dictionary, or drawing out complicated concepts into a graph that makes sense to you visually. Oftentimes if we can "see" words in picture form with our eyes, it becomes easier to grasp its meaning. In other words, enjoy the Scriptures! They were written for us to comprehend and apply. So, spend time grappling with the Good Book!

The Word-a-Week Workout. Take one word that stays with you during Bible reading, devotion, or meditation and develop an entire research paper on it. Become an expert on one-word studies like: *Father, faith, church, Christian, love, the Holy Spirit, mammon, flesh,* or *believe.* The Bible is full of hidden treasures, and a committed and skilled "workman" will dig deep enough and long enough to strike gold. True riches await. Start with one word!

Weekend Meditation and Reflection. At the end of a busy week, periodically schedule a weekend adventure with the Lord to simply meditate and reflect on where you've come from, where you are, and where you're going. The best way to begin is to start reading God's written revelation to man—the Bible. Read until the sizzle of the match of God's message ignites your heart. When a verse burns with personal relevance, you will feel it strongly. As you reach that place of passion, simply stop and meditate. Meditation involves reviewing various thoughts by mulling them over in your mind and heart. When you take deliberate time to deeply consider a scriptural truth, God's Word will vitally affect how you live, grow, and walk with God. It is here that the Lord wants to reveal some things to you. So, be still.

A Monthly Retreat of Silence. With all of the constant hustle and bustle of life, Black Christian women need a time and place to be silent. No yelling at the kids, chatting with the girls, or counseling your neighbor. It's a call for a "tongue rest." That means no talking allowed. A retreat of silence is an extended period of time in which a person seeks seclusion away from the world. There is no man-made noise or other human being with whom to converse. The purpose of this retreat is to:

- be alone with the Lord of Life
- rest in His arms
- bring Him the pleasure of your full attention
- meditate on Scripture concerning stillness (Psalms 37:7; 46:10; 62:1; Zephaniah 1:7; and Zechariah 2:13)
- refresh your soul and spirit

Only a Bible and notebook are necessary. All other books and reading materials should be left for another time. Often included in a retreat of silence is a nature walk or hike in the woods. It's a time to clear your head and empty your heart so that you can hear from heaven. There is barrenness in busyness and numbness in noise that takes its toll on us as spiritual beings. This kind of monthly retreat will fortify your soul. Once we are nourished and continually nurtured, we will become better able to aid, assist, and serve others in need.

Encouraging Ourselves and Others in the Word

Years ago I learned a powerful definition for the word *encourage*. It means "to give courage to another to do what is right." Through a lifetime of trials and testing, I have come to know our Father, Papa God (my own personal endearment) as the ultimate encourager. His Word gives us enormous courage and capacity to change and navigate the circumstances around us. Instead of drowning in a cesspool of negative facts and stinking realities, we can boldly and courageously speak God's Word. God has given us the ability to proclaim His truth that transforms lives, alters situations, and creates new opportunities.

Queen Esther is a perfect example of having the courage to do right. Her bold proclamation, *"If I perish, I perish"* (Esther 4:16), is "not fatalistic nor a declaration of resignation," according to the editors of the *African American Lectionary*, "but a statement of theological defiance and fundamental belief in the divine providence in her life. The statement exudes a spiritual wisdom that affirms that to perish while standing up for what is right is to be reborn into the life of the spirit.

"It is a statement of the deepest faith and confidence in the interruption and interference of God in her life to continue to live spiritually in God even if the King kills her physically." In verses 15–17, the divine intervention and interruption in Esther's spirit moved her from being a "passive beauty queen and royal ornament to an active agent of change." Not only does she nurture her own self but moves swiftly to involve the entire community by imploring them to fast and pray. She is encouraged deep within. Her faith and courageous spirit is empowering to others (*African American Lectionary*, September 2008).

Courage to Walk in Faith

Possessing a strong and courageous spirit is part of our legacy as Black Christian women. We must continue the legacy of the godly women who have gone before us. They relied not only on public image, outer beauty, intellect, talents, or leadership skills alone but persevered through trials by standing on a firm foundation of faith. We must be determined, as our predecessors were, to submit to the leading of the Holy Spirit and remain poised for progressive action. Whenever the Lord sends a word of instruction, correction, or direction, we must offer Him a God-fearing heart that is ready to obey His command. By nurturing our inner-self through the study of God's Holy Word,

we are empowered to walk in obedience!

As we nurture our spiritual selves and become deeply rooted in the Word and the will of God, we become hometown missionaries with an objective that is life-enhancing in our personal lives and expansive in our ability to influence and assist others. As a result of our spiritual depth, we are equipped and compelled by the Holy Spirit to be agents of transformation in the lives of those around us. Our sensitivity to the will of God, as confirmed in His Word, gives women of God a keen awareness of the needs and issues of those in our circle of friends and realm of influence. We can share the gospel with those around us in a more relevant, meaningful, and personalized manner.

Pursuit of Maturity to Help Others Grow

There are many challenges and areas of sin and brokenness that Black women disproportionately face. I recently encountered an Internet chat that revealed a very sad heart. The message rings through loud and clear, signifying the vital need for spiritual nurture among women, both Christian and non-Christian. Perhaps some of us have been in similar shoes and can relate to the depth of such anguish:

> When I was growing up and going to Sunday school, I used to hate when the teacher asked what our talents were. I remember saying that God didn't give me one. Now that I am a thirty-four-year-old woman, well, I do have a decent job. Thank God. I feel like I am too late with life—as if I fell behind and that I didn't turn out the way I wanted to turn out. I don't want to end up drinking a lot again and Lord knows I am struggling to quit smoking. It feels like my only comfort. I look at other women like my mother and my sister. I feel as if I do not measure up. They know how to dress and they have a certain sense of self; even the women on the street do too. I believe when people meet my mother or my sister they like them more. I feel as if they don't like me at all. I feel like the odd girl out. I used to be saved, but I didn't walk the narrow path too long. I have been prayed for and I have prayed for deliverance a lot. I feel as if my generation is cursed. I am depressed again. Oh, Lord, forgive me when I say this, but I attempted suicide almost six years ago and at times I wish it was a success. But I couldn't do it because it's a sin. I don't know . . . This life

is rough. I always wanted to be this well-admired person . . .

—African American Spirituality, AOL Black Voices, October 9, 2008

We must become our sister's keeper, sharing the good news of Christ's love and forgiveness. We don't want to stop there, however. We have the unique opportunity to impact families, cities, and ultimately our nation and the world with answers to many of life's challenges. The solutions to the dilemmas of life are contained in the Word of God. As Christian women, we must learn to effectively address critical life issues, using the Bible as our instruction manual. Gandhi posed it very wisely: we must "live the change we want to see." Your life (and mine) may be the only Scripture many people ever read! Our spiritual nourishment and biblical fortitude is crucial and will make us the "threshing instrument" necessary to raise up a generation of healed, redeemed, and powerful women for the kingdom of God.

Every one of us who tends faithfully to our own personal sanctuary and stokes the internal fire of the Holy Spirit can become an instant "flame" to ignite the hearts of other women who remain outside the warm, saving grace of Christ. As Isaiah 50:4 states, "*The Sovereign Lord has given me an instructed tongue to know the word that sustains the weary. He wakens me morning by morning, wakens my ear to listen like one being taught.*" And so it is, we learn that nurturing the "inner life" and spirit is not about us alone. It's always about God and others.

In her book *It's Not about You—It's about God*, Rebecca Florence Osaigbovo (2004) reminds us:

When most of us give our lives to God, our biggest consideration is what we will receive . . . Teachings that keep us with God are laden with promises of health, peace, success, happiness, prosperity and the answers to all our problems. Well, I'm not going to burst your bubble. I believe all of the above and more are true. However, if that's all you desire in life, you need look no further. [But] if you're like some people I know, perhaps you are bored with the status quo . . . God is giving you an invitation to purposely live your life on a higher plane. He desires your permission to demonstrate his ways through your life. If you do say yes to his invitation, know up front that no matter what you have gone through and may yet go

through, it really is not about you . . . We need to begin to understand life from God's perspective. (Osaigbovo 2004)

MAKING SURE OUR ANCHOR HOLDS

Avoiding New Age Pitfalls

As we look at the powerful anchor of the Christian faith, we must return to the "old landmark" that is outlined in the Holy Scriptures. God told His people in Hosea 5:10 that *"Judah's leaders are like those who move boundary stones. I will pour out my wrath on them like a flood of water."* God had erected spiritual boundaries and mental markings around His chosen people. His Holy Word was to be their landmark of conviction and direction that helped them discern right from wrong. Because they removed the boundaries God had established, God was not pleased. As we look at secular spirituality today, red flags of warning flash incessantly before us. We must not ignore the warnings but take heed to the Holy Spirit who is ever ready to guide us into all truth.

According to Wikipedia, the New Age phenomena represent "a perceived sense of connection [which] forms a central defining characteristic of spirituality—connection to a metaphysical reality greater than oneself, which may include an emotional experience of religious awe and reverence." Clearly, there is nothing in this definition that bespeaks authentic faith in the living Lord, as He is revealed in our Judeo-Christian faith.

In his article for Christian Information Ministries, Russ Wise summarizes the disturbing trend he exposes as postmodern evangelism this way:

The Bible is clear in its teaching that God is not an impersonal "it" or energy/force. God is triune, a personal Being who cares for His creation, and a Creator who governs the universe rather than an energy that encompasses it. Jesus is not a way-shower, but The Way. He is God incarnate and our redemption; He is our salvation. Salvation does not come to man through personal enlightenment or recognizing one's innate divinity; it comes by man's obedience to a holy and just God who sacrificed Himself for their souls. All religions are not equal. They are not various paths by which man can travel to reach his own perfection. Jesus is unique and therefore Christianity is truly the only way to man's salvation as understood by Jesus' resurrection. No other religious leader or guru has risen from the dead. Jesus alone accomplished it. Without the gospel of His saving grace man cannot be worthy to stand before a righteous God and escape without condemnation. Jesus is the final judge of mankind. Man will not be able to gather enough positive energy on that day to alter the course. The time for right choices is now. There will not be another opportunity in the afterlife. (Wise, CIM website 2005)

Do not be deceived. We cannot be hoodwinked or bamboozled by the false prophets of this modern era and succumb to the pitfalls of their heresies, lest we be led away from God Almighty. The Scriptures are clear that *"until heaven and earth disappear, not the smallest letter, not the least stroke of a pen, will by any means disappear from the Law"* (Matthew 5:18). If we are going to make sure that our anchor holds, we must hold to God's unchanging hand. We must never forsake the way of holiness and righteousness that is provided through the death, burial, resurrection, and triumphant ascension of Christ Jesus our Lord. Furthermore, as we work to build God's kingdom, it is our duty as Christian believers to lead others to the truth of God's Word of salvation.

ANCHOR STRATEGIES FOR WOMEN OF FAITH

Leaning on the Lord in a New Millennium

> *We've come this far by faith*
> *Leaning on the Lord*
> *Trusting in His holy word*
> *He's never failed me yet*
> *No turning around*
> *We've come this far by faith.*

—"WE'VE COME THIS FAR"; COMPOSER: ALBERT A. GOODSON, 1956

Black Christian women have the opportunity to show the world our anchor. People are looking for life's answers in this restless and often unfriendly culture. They find themselves characterized by the unreliable and unstable nature of this world that cannot confirm their significance. All the while we possess the solution to a culture that leaves them wandering aimlessly and lacking a life purpose. We have found what they need: the security and stability that is missing in life. We must tell them that they need a firm foundation, an anchor. And that anchor is Jesus Christ!

The strategies for modern women of God have not been altered or changed from the "old school" or "old path" we were taught early on. These are the anchors that hold us firmly in Christ. They have brought us this far along the way, and they will take us all the way home. Let's herald them for a final spiritual showcase:

- We must hold on to our **saving faith in Jesus Christ as Redeemer and Deliverer.** He is the Way, Truth, and Life. There is not another!
- There is no alternative for having an **uncompromising belief in God's Holy Word.** This requires that we study the Bible and learn its precepts, commandments, and instructions for successful living. For a fresh perspective, try keeping a journal in which you record how God speaks prophetically and directly to you through strong impressions you find in His Word. This is like mining for treasure or going on an adventurous journey.
- **Uttering prayers with unshakable trust** moves mountains and reconstructs landscapes. It has been the power source of the Christian faith since Jesus taught the disciples to pray, "Our Father, in heaven." A tangible way to personalize your prayers would be to write them out like prose or poems. For the creative and artistic, this could be deeply gratifying. Personalizing the Word by putting your name in the text is another way to expand your dimension of prayer and create an energetic atmosphere for practicing your faith. Try it and enjoy the liberty that personal conversations with God will provide for you.
- Don't ever forget the intimacy that comes from **worship and singing songs, hymns, and spiritual songs.** Music is a powerful medium. It can calm a raging storm in the heart and speak peace to mental turmoil. God enjoys hearing the melodic sounds of our praise. So, when life is tough, sing, because God is always good!

CONCLUSION

God has called us into a spiritual relationship with Him that is awe-inspiring and continually thrilling. As Black Christian women, we stand in a special place of serving the King of kings and the Lord of lords with everything we have, whether little or much. Our lives do not consist in the things we possess but in the Person who possesses us! He has provided an anchor for us that is firm and secure through Christ Jesus.

A strong legacy of faith has been passed down to us and we cannot deny the love of Christ, the power of the cross, or the supernatural protection and assistance God has afforded us down through the years. Life has not always been easy or prosperous for us as a cultural group, but through the Spirit-empowered life, we have obtained an anchor of the soul that is not easily moved. Spiritually, we have received a legacy that is extremely valuable and we must now faithfully pass it on. So, be empowered by the Spirit of God and our Lord Jesus Christ—a true anchor of the soul!

REFERENCES

African American Spirituality, Our Daily Bread, Do we all have talent? Message boards, Chats and Profiles. AOL Black Voices, October 9, 2008. http://www.blackvoices.com/boards/spirituality/upperroom/our-daily-bread/do-we-all-have-talent/15972/printDisc/1/20.

Kellerman, Robert, W. 2005. *Soul Physicians: A Theology of Soul Care and Spiritual Direction.* Taneytown, Maryland: RPM Books, p.126.

NegroSpirituals.com. This section organized by Spiritual Workshop, Paris, France. http://www.negrospirituals.com/.

Osaigbovo, Rebecca Florence. 2004. *It's Not about You—It's about God.* Downers Grove, Illinois: InterVarsity Press.

Powell, Yolanda, and William J. Powell. 2003. *Soul Food & Living Water: Spiritual Nourishment and Practical Help for African American Families.* Focus on the Family & Chicago: Moody Publishers.

Taylor, Jack. 1999. *Hallelujah Factor.* Revised edition. Mansfield, Pennsylvania: Kingdom Publishing.

The African American Lectionary, Sunday, September 14, 2008. http://www.theafricanamericanlectionary.org/PopupLectionaryReading.asp?LRID=43.

White, Michelle D. "African American Christian Spirituality in the Face of Illness." *The Yale Journal for Humanities in Medicine* (Published: May 9, 2002). http://yjhm.yale.edu/archives/spirit2003/faith/mwhite.htm.

Wikipedia, http://en.wikipedia.org/wiki/Spirituality, last modified March 22, 2009.

Wise, Russ. "Oprah Winfrey: The Oprahfication of America—The Impact of a Postmodern Evangelist." Article published on *Christian Information Ministries Website* (November 23, 2005). http://www.christianinformation.org/article.asp?artID=103.

Chapter Two

SHE SHALL BE CALLED
WOMAN: EMBRACING
WHO GOD SAYS I AM

Now it is God who makes both us and you stand firm in Christ. He anointed us, set his seal of ownership on us, and put his Spirit in our hearts as a deposit, guaranteeing what is to come.

2 CORINTHIANS 1:21–22

Sabrina D. Black

"*Who am I?* Why am I here? Where did I come from? Why am I a part of this family, a citizen of this country? Why this period of history?" Do these questions sound familiar to you? Self-concept is our search for significance, for meaning and purpose in life. "What am I supposed to do with my life? Do I have any skills? Do I have any abilities? Am I gifted in any way?"

And, there are still more questions: "Do people really care about me? Would it matter if I were not here? Would anyone miss me if I wasn't here? What will be said about me when I'm gone? Will I leave a mark in this world?"

Many of us struggle and wrestle with our identity as daughters of the Most High. It is my sincere hope that by the end of our discussion in this chapter, we will arrive at a place where we rest in God regarding our identity. Thank God that His Word has answers to our many questions regarding who we are and why we are here!

Our self-concept gradually emerges in the early months of life. What we believe about ourselves and the intrinsic value we place on our worth and worthiness as individuals is shaped and significantly affected by family, friends, and the larger culture. These effects continue through childhood and progress throughout our entire lives. In other words, our self-concept is the sum total of the knowledge we "bank" over the years combined with the behaviors, the "dividends" of many things we have become convinced of about our personhood and value. All of this together forms our concept of who we are—individually and collectively as part of the larger society.

HOW IS OUR SENSE OF SELF CONCEPTUALIZED?

A person's perception of herself is often defined by the role she plays in her community; that is, what she *does*. For example, a woman may define herself as a mother, sister, friend, housekeeper, teacher, nurse, or by some other task or responsibility she may have.

When children are developing and we characterize them by what they *do* versus who they *are*, we begin to shape the image and perspective they have of themselves. Therefore, children should not be called "bad boys" or "bad girls." Instead, as parents and caregivers, we must learn to identify and emphasize that it is the misbehavior that is unacceptable, not the child herself.

It is vital that children understand they are loved unconditionally. When we love the Lord, we want to obey His will and make sure that we are meeting our children's need for love. Part of Mom and Dad's desire should be that the children God has entrusted to them will be conformed to the character of Christ. Furthermore, parents must be committed to helping them achieve that goal. We should speak into existence those things we want to see formed in the lives of our children. An example of this would be to say, "You are not a liar, so you must only tell Mommy the truth. Telling lies is not a good thing to do."

One Girl's Journey

Our self-concept is greatly affected by the era in which we were born. The experience of those born prior to the 1960s is in stark contrast to women born after that period. Little girls who grew up before the civil rights movement lived in a different culture—a seemingly different country for that matter! Girls, in general, and Black girls in particular, were limited in regard to what they could do. Roles were very narrowly defined. Most Black girls could only hope to become mothers, teachers, or domestics. All of these roles are admirable and extremely important to our communities, but they also represent the limits imposed by society previous to the civil rights movement. Today, the aspirations of Black women and our daughters are only limited by what we can dream!

Della remembers growing up in the South, just before the civil rights movement. Life was hard and cruel for Black Americans across the nation, but most especially in the Deep South. Listen to her words:

As a young Black girl I had to struggle to hold on to my positive self-concept. Families were larger then, usually nine or more children. Boys were more valued than girls, and light-skinned girls considered prettier than dark-skinned girls. And if a light-skinned girl had long curly hair, she was considered the prettiest of all, almost as valued as boys. Physical appearance played a major role in regard to how children were esteemed by family, at school, in the church, and in the community.

My mother took care to offset the negative experiences I had in my world. She told me that I was smart and pretty. I wanted to believe her, but I was not convinced because actions speak so much louder than words. My grammar and Sunday school teachers all picked the lighter children to receive special privileges and recognition. When I and the other darker complexioned children objected and became sullen, refusing to talk, and temperamental, we were disciplined for our antisocial behavior and inability to cooperate cheerfully; we were reprimanded with remarks like "beauty is as beauty does."

You can imagine what that did for my self-concept. I was frequently told, however subtle the suggestion, through the preferential treatment that I never received, that I had to work harder at doing good to be accepted—because I was nappy headed and dark. Ugly. After all, what else could I conclude? I lived in a dull gray world full of the clouds of self-doubt and contempt, contrived by the hazy fog of rejection. My heart still hurts and tears sting my eyes remembering the rejection heaped on me. Rejection that I received as part of my race, once by living in a society that practiced legally endorsed discrimination, then twice—the most painful of all—being rejected by those within my own community.

Many dark-skinned women from that era can tell similar horror stories of their unique trials and desire to be accepted, appreciated, and valued. In her book *Hurt People Hurt People: Hope and Healing for Yourself and Your Relationships,* Dr. Sandra Wilson (2001) talks about how the wounds and distorted images from childhood affect and inhibit our ability to nurture ourselves, our children, and other loved ones. Ultimately, we hurt others because of our own pain. Perhaps this explains, in large part, why those who were victimized by the same rejection in regard to racism and skin color would themselves reject and deeply hurt innocent children (Wilson 2001).

Della's story resonates in the hearts of those who have had similar experiences. We all have a story to tell, whether we identify with Della or the light-skinned, curly haired girls. The way we were treated in childhood and the voices that we valued and listened to helped shape our perspective of who we are and how we measure and interpret our significance in the world.

Fortunately, these attitudes about skin color are finally changing. African Americans have proven to be substantial consumers, spending millions of dollars annually on cosmetics and hair care products, not to mention toys for our children. Our formidable market has required that manufacturers and retailers provide items that are reflective of the beauty in our race of numerous hues.

In recent years, we can find women who are more representative of our diversity in advertisements and on television. It isn't difficult to go to a department or toy store today and find a gorgeous, chocolate-colored doll with which our little girls can play. Hopefully, this cultural and societal "revelation"—that beauty comes in all colors—can help heal the hurts that were inflicted on women like Della.

I am excited about sharing with you the difference between God's system of self-evaluation and man's. But first I would like to briefly encourage you to consider the responsibility and power that we have as adults in the lives of children to ensure that they develop a healthy, wholesome attitude about themselves. It is our duty to help them be receptive to the further truths of God's Word in regard to self-concept.

The Power of a Parent's Perspective

My parents were committed to me becoming something more and greater than what society thought possible for a skinny little dark-skinned girl growing up in the early sixties. This was just before the time when James Brown declared "I'm Black and I'm proud" in 1968.

What's in a Name?

Since self-concept is formed by the words we hear, it would stand to reason that the names we choose to give our children hold great significance. When God wanted to change Abram's *perception* (his thoughts about himself) and his *prospects* (his thoughts about his life's work and purpose), He changed his name to Abraham, which means "father of many nations." His new name identified his purpose in God. Sarai's name was changed to Sarah, which means "beloved princess." Perhaps this name change for Sarah was to help her know that her Father God, the King of kings, would not forsake or forget her. She was His beloved and she need not fear her future (Genesis 17:1–22).

Every time Abraham and Sarah were beckoned by their new names, God was whispering to them that they would be changed from a barren couple to the father and mother of many nations. Despite the fact that Abraham and Sarah made many choices indicating they forgot the promises of God inherent in their new identities, God was faithful and kept His promise to them. And their descendants are "as numerous as the stars" (Genesis 22:16–18).

However, naming children today does not hold the same significance that it did during biblical times. Many contemporary parents make the mistake of giving their children names with no meaning, purpose, or vision of who they will become. Yet, our African ancestors were very intentional about naming children. They gave their children names like "Precious," "Praise," and "Pearl." Each of those names attaches great value and worth to the daughter who owns one of them.

When my father named me Sabrina, he was very intentional. I was named after the German airline Sabena and my name means "one who will soar the heights and know no limits." The Latin origin of Sabrina means "peaceful warrior" or "one who battles on her knees." I've always liked my name. My parents often reminded me that I could do anything, go anywhere, and have an array of wonderful experiences because I was destined for success.

Parents as Advocates and Teachers

I remember my mother coming to the school on a regular basis to confer with my teacher regarding some untruth the school system was attempting to impart or some limitation an educator was trying to impose on me. For example, my penmanship posed a problem for one particular teacher.

I was so proud to be a leftie like my dad. We were unique and could do something that most others couldn't do. Dad had great penmanship and we would spend time in the evenings doing homework and writing stories. My dad read stories to me about famous left-handed people, like James Baldwin, Lewis Carroll, Mark Twain, Cole Porter, Lou Rawls, Michelangelo, Leonardo da Vinci, and Henry Ford. Dad talked proudly about how creative we were because *left-handed* people are in their *right mind*!

Mrs. Branch (my tall, slender, young White teacher with a bouffant hairdo), however, thought it was wrong that I did not write with my right hand. My knuckles and the palms of my hands were red from the swats of her ruler as she tried to insist that I conform to the "norm" of the other students in class and the larger society. Well, my mother told Mrs. Branch in no uncertain terms that as long as she could read my writing, I could write with whatever hand I chose. My mom's willingness to advocate for me did wonders for my self-concept (along with the many other times my parents met with Mrs. Branch).

As evidenced by my experience and Della's, teachers are very important people in the lives of their students. They spend more time with children than almost anyone else in a child's circle of influence. As a result, teachers should be aware of the importance of the impact they have on a student's self-concept. It is even more vital for parents to acknowledge the power and influence of teachers over their children and pay close attention to those critical relationships.

In fact, it is crucial for parents to be involved and active in the educational experience of their children. Deuteronomy 6:6–7 exhorts parents in regard to their responsibility and importance in the lives of their children: "*These commandments that I give you today are to be upon your hearts. Impress them on your children. Talk about them when you sit at home and when you walk along the road, when you lie down and when you get up.*"

These verses adamantly imply that as parents, we should be aware of the environments our children are in and the subsequent influences of their surroundings at all times. Ideally, parents are a child's primary teacher. During the last decade, the home education movement has grown greatly because parents have come to acknowledge and embrace this responsibility. As children are constantly shaping and reshaping their identities, it is our job to help them recognize their strengths and to ensure that they consistently view themselves in a positive light.

Whether we choose to home educate or delegate that authority to the traditional classroom education system, ultimately, God will hold us responsible for what happens to our children during the years they must rely on us for care and protection.

Who Does God Say We Are?

Cognitive theory is the study of how our thought processes are developed. Research by cognitive theorists demonstrates what God's Word confirms: When we repeat in our minds the messages sent to us by the actions of others that make us feel uncomfortable about who we are, those negative, uncomfortable messages lead to negative self-talk. Such adverse communication then leads to irrational thinking regarding oneself and the world. Talk about the proverbial row of falling dominoes! To combat this negativity from taking hold of our lives, we must turn to Scripture and abide by the mandate in Romans 12:2: *"Do not conform any longer to the pattern of this world, but be transformed by the renewing of your mind."*

There is a new awareness on the part of both lay and professional counselors that strongly suggests that self-concept cannot be ignored. If we are to successfully address nagging problems, including drug and alcohol abuse, high school dropout rates, dysfunction in our families, and other psychosocial dilemmas, the self-concept of an individual must first be examined.

Dysfunction arises when we are not secure and stable in regard to our identity; we need a loving community to surround us. When we lack a nurturing community that allows us to grow with the freedom to discover and even reinvent who we are, then we are challenged by and become vulnerable to the pressures of society-at-large. The temptation to become who others think we are may be compounded by our isolation, allowing someone other than the authority of God's Word to define our worth and personhood.

In fact, our self-concept will be a meaningful determinant in the course of our lives. This recognition should motivate us to stop and take a look at who we really are in Christ, according to God's Word, as opposed to who we perceive ourselves to be based on the thoughts or opinions of others. It makes all the difference when we see ourselves through the eyes of God's love and form our self-concept around His thoughts of us. God loved and valued us so much that He gave His Son on our behalf. The Son of God loved and valued us enough to lay down His life for us! Who we are matters greatly to God; therefore, we receive a far greater benefit in basing our opinions of ourselves on how God sees us.

Being loved by the God of the universe helps us to esteem ourselves and others highly. Since our self-concept revolves around who we think we are, let's think and believe what God says about us in His Word. He has established this truth about man: *"For as he thinketh in his heart, so is he"* (Proverbs 23:7a KJV). The following list, compiled by Neil Anderson and included in his book *The Bondage Breaker* (2006) is a great way to begin embracing our true identity in Christ. Whose report shall you believe? As for me, I will believe the report of the Lord! And God says that I am:

- His child (John 1:12)
- Christ's friend (John 15:15)
- United with the Lord in spirit (1 Corinthians 6:17)
- Bought with a price (1 Corinthians 6:19–20)
- A saint, set apart for God (Ephesians 1:1)
- A personal witness of Christ (Acts 1:8)
- The salt and light of the earth (Matthew 5:13–14)
- A member of the body of Christ (1 Corinthians 12:27)
- Free forever from condemnation (Romans 8:1–2)
- A citizen of heaven (Philippians 3:20)
- Free from any charge against me (Romans 8:31–34)
- A minister of reconciliation for God (2 Corinthians 5:17–21)
- Seated with Christ in the heavenly realms (Ephesians 2:6)
- Established, anointed, and sealed by God (2 Corinthians 1:21–22)
- Assured that all things work together for my good (Romans 8:28)
- God's temple (1 Corinthians 3:16)
- Hidden with Christ in God (Colossians 3:3)
- Complete in Christ (Colossians 2:10)
- Justified by faith (Romans 5:1)
- God's co-worker (1 Corinthians 3:9; 2 Corinthians 6:1)
- God's workmanship (Ephesians 2:10)
- Confident that the good work God has begun in me will be perfected (Philippians 1:5–6)
- Redeemed and forgiven (Colossians 1:14)

Further, God says:

- I have access to God through the Holy Spirit (Ephesians 2:18).
- I cannot be separated from the love of God (Romans 8:35–39).

* I have been chosen and appointed to bear fruit (John 15:16).
* I may approach God with freedom and confidence (Ephesians 3:12).
* I can do all things through Christ who strengthens me (Philippians 4:13).
* I have been adopted as God's child (Ephesians 1:5). (Anderson 2006)

Try reading this list of truths every day for a month, preferably out loud. It will help transform any faulty, negative beliefs about who you are and help you embrace your true identity in Christ.

WHY IS SELF-CONCEPT SO POWERFUL IN DETERMINING THE COURSE OF ONE'S LIFE?

Successes and failures in many areas of life are closely related to the way people have learned to view themselves and their relationships with others. There are numerous factors that also have a direct relation to our sense of self-value and self-esteem. It has become clear that self-concept has many qualities. From my years of study and experience with helping others to develop a healthy sense of self, I have identified at least three major descriptive qualities of self-concept that can be defined as: Acquired, Arranged, and Active.

Quality #1—Self-Concept Is ACQUIRED

In trying to understand how we arrive at our self-concept, consider this formula: all of life's encounters, plus our experiences, multiplied by our positive exchanges, equals enhanced self-esteem. From previous experiences and present perceptions, we form opinions of ourselves. We see ourselves sometimes totally different from the ways others see us. As a result, if we want to change our life in any way, we need to know ourselves before we can act. We need to determine what we must do to head in the right direction and we can't do that until we know ourselves. Moreover, the knowledge we acquire about who we are not only comes from external forces but more importantly from the voice within—the voice that is God in us calling us to our destiny.

As young girls learn to believe and dare to dream, they will hear their own heartbeats and drumbeats and follow the path that God has for them. They need to be taught that when negative information about who they are is presented, they do not have to receive it. At times like these, there is usually a voice within that strongly disagrees. But all of us need to understand that becoming self-aware doesn't mean we are being selfish. Rather, when a young lady discovers who she really is, she will be able to give more of herself to others and that will benefit her interpersonal relationships as well as help build her self-esteem.

Becoming self-aware is an ongoing process of authenticity and genuineness. We need to make it a priority to get to know who we really are—our dreams, achievements, strengths, and weaknesses. I believe that challenges (even rejection) in life help make us more aware of who we are and whose we are, so that we can develop a keener sense of what is most important to us. The way we respond to our own physical, mental, social, and spiritual development is acquired based on our exposure to God's Word and to people who reinforce what His Word has to say. We perceive different aspects of ourselves at different times with varying degrees of clarity.

Therefore, inner focusing is a valuable tool for counseling those who are looking to develop a healthy self-concept. In the woman's role of nurturer, take this knowledge to heart personally and teach your daughters in a way to help them acquire their own positive self-concept.

Quality #2—Self-Concept Is ARRANGED

All of our encounters, experiences, and life exchanges are arranged in our memory banks in a way that is consistent with the image that we believe; they are a reflection of who we are and are destined to become. It is not a strange phenomenon that Black women can survive the toughest experiences yet survive with great resilience. It is the sequencing of life events and the meaning that we attribute to each that becomes a building block upon which we stand, from which we step, and from which we soar.

However, our basic perceptions of who we are remain quite stable, so change takes time. For example, when despite life's circumstances I view myself as destined for greatness, delivered from evil, and determined to achieve, then I am not distracted by what others have to say or who they think I am because I already know. Most researchers agree that self-concept has a generally stable quality that is characterized by orderliness and harmony. Each person maintains countless perceptions regarding their personal existence, and each perception is orchestrated with all the others. It is this fluid arrangement of thought regarding our self-concept that is generally stable and organized that brings a consistent quality to our personalities.

Self-concept requires stability and tends to resist change. This is also true in reverse. When young Black girls are negatively impacted by racism, feminism, and classism as well as other "isms" of society, and they are not able to arrange a construct for these views that tells them something different about themselves, then they become the sum of those voices. If self-concept changed readily, we would lack a consistent and dependable personality. The more central a particular belief is to our self-concept, the more resistant we are to changing that belief.

For example, when we encounter a sister who has had a negative experience with society, it is important to help her renew her mind in accordance with the Word of God. When her mind is rearranged to include God's thoughts first and last, realizing that He is the author and finisher of her faith, then she will be able to arrange a healthy self-concept.

Quality #3—Self-Concept Is ACTIVE

To understand the active nature of self-concept, it helps to imagine it as a continuously dynamic system that grows and expands to encompass a person's perceived existence. This not only shapes the ways that a person views oneself, others, and the world, but it also serves to direct action and enables each individual to take a consistent "stance" in life. Rather than viewing self-concept as the cause of behavior, it is better understood as providing consistency in personality and direction for behavior. The active quality of self-concept is always evolving natural consequences and/or benefits and rewards. Listed below are four views of this active nature of self-concept:

1. *Systematic*—The world and the things in it are not just perceived in a generic sense, they are perceived in relation to one's self-concept. The event or the circumstance is not the determining factor; it relates to how an incident impacts the individual. This partially explains how siblings grow up in the same home environment with the same parents yet process the impact of events differently and come to conclusions about their own identity based on the effect a given situation has on each child.

2. *Sequential*—Self-concept development is a continuous process. In the healthy personality, there is constant assimilation of new ideas and expulsion of old ideas throughout life. As the individual develops and becomes more of who they are internally, by design, they are able to release the world's view of who they are not. This process of "put offs" and "put ons" of a proper self-image grows over time.

3. *Symmetric*—Individuals strive to behave in ways that are in keeping with their self-concepts, no matter how helpful or hurtful to themselves or others. Each individual will seek to be balanced in their thoughts and actions that pertain to who they are in the world.

4. *Substantive*—Self-concept usually takes precedence over the physical body. Individuals will often sacrifice physical comfort and safety for emotional satisfaction. Physical body image has a great impact on our self-esteem even though many may think in superficial terms. More than anything, young girls want to assimilate and fit in; they do not want to stand out from the group. Consequently, they will go to great lengths to minimize or maximize physical features based on what is perceived as "acceptable."

Our self-concept has everything to do with how we feel and think about ourselves. Recently, I saw a movie that is a perfect example of this point. It was an old movie classic from 1945, entitled *The Enchanted Cottage,* starring Dorothy McGuire and Robert Young. As the story goes, a homely maid and a scarred ex-GI meet at the cottage where she works and where he was to spend his honeymoon prior to being injured in an accident. The two develop a bond and agree to marry, although their decision is more out of loneliness than love.

The romantic spirit of the cottage, however, begins to overtake them. They soon start to look beautiful to each other, but not to anyone else. At first, the lonely woman was obviously not attractive to the battle-scarred man or to the audience. He was burned, scarred, and repulsive-looking to everyone. But, once they began honestly interacting with each other, the audience was allowed to accept them as real, humble, and friendly people.

When the clever film director had the makeup crew ever so slowly begin to soften their features, it made the characters' formerly perceived homeliness and ugliness more and more transparent. Thus, the couple began to fall deeper in love as they began to see the other as the person they had sought after for so long.

The audience witnessed the change too! Eventually, their true beauty became very apparent; both of them were satisfied with the other's attractiveness. The audience and the female player saw the male actor as a most handsome man and she was a vision of loveliness. It was a moment to be remembered.

I believe it was one of the most inspiring "happenings" I've ever witnessed on film. Two scarred people are transformed by love while living in a very special cottage. It's so good to be able to recall that moment so vividly. The power of love cannot be overestimated. Our self-esteem is tied up with our being accepted and loved unconditionally. What is beauty? Beauty is truly in the eyes of the beholder. As the characters that McGuire and Young portrayed began to accept and love each other, all the plainness and repulsiveness melted away and through the eyes of love—they were beautiful.

What Is Beauty?

Whatever we think and believe about ourselves is our reality. Because our perspectives shape our world, we behave in accordance with what we believe about ourselves. So many of our young people and older ones too have warped self-images because of what they are and are told is beautiful, or smart, or chic in today's society. It really doesn't even make a difference if you are "all that and a bag of chips." If you believe in your heart that you are ugly, in your mind you are ugly, and no person or mirror can convince you otherwise.

There are those who are dying of starvation because when they look in the mirror, they see themselves as fat, even though, in reality they are only skin and bones. You may notice a tall, slender young girl walking with her shoulders rounded and hunched over so that she doesn't appear as tall. Believe it or not, others strap their breasts down to not appear big busted. Some have corns on their toes from squeezing their feet into shoes one or two sizes too small. When, in fact, the anguish we experience would vanish if we learned to accept the way God made us.

Young girls need to be reminded that the Lord God formed and fashioned them in their mothers' wombs. He knows everything about them. Therefore, mothers with young girls offer enormous support to their daughters when they teach them how valuable they are in God's eyes. As part of a mother's role in guiding her children's destiny, it is extremely important for her to help them to understand their self-worth.

Our perceptions are conditioned by our environmental and cultural heritage. And what we conceive of as beautiful in one area of the world may not be seen as beautiful in another area. As a result, American culture has warped our ideas of beauty and worth. For African Americans, this has caused a shift in our values from the internal to the external. But I remember my first trip to Africa when I discovered something very different. I was amazed at the number of very dark-skinned people that I encountered. Their complexion is what we might describe as "black-blue." And it was a beautiful sight. This was one time that I was not the darkest one in the room.

Our self-concept is thought to have three components: physical appearance (how we look externally), character (internal beauty), and our behavior (how we treat others). Yet, so many women are obsessed with only one—their outward appearance. Oddly enough, other cultures are now paying good money to get the features and appointments that Black women have always had: large, full lips, voluptuous breasts, broad shoulders, wide hips, and braided hair. It's amazing that when the Caucasian actress Bo Derek braided her hair, she became a "10" on the scale of loveliness.

It wasn't until this event occurred that braids were considered chic. Botox and collagen have become staples as other races seek to acquire the features of Black women. Yet many of us still fail to see the beauty in our afrocentric attributes. As we help young Black girls embrace all three of the elements of real beauty, we can help reinforce the adage of Della's mother, "beauty is as beauty does." There is much truth in that statement.

I am sure all of us know people or remember acquaintances who were not so attractive but had great personalities. Somehow we overlooked their less-than-perfect physical appearance because we saw the sincerity of their heart. As we encourage young girls to embrace all the aspects of beauty, we must teach them to embrace the Scripture in Proverbs 31:30. It reminds us that *"charm is deceptive, and beauty is fleeting; but a woman who fears the Lord is to be praised."* In order to achieve true success in life, young girls must learn that it is the character of Christ that makes a person truly beautiful. And it is our responsibility as mothers and mentors to ensure that they know what God's Word has to say about them. We also need to remind them that their bodies are the temple of the living God.

Every temple should be well-kept, well-groomed, and well-cared for. We have to make sure that girls understand what this means in their personal lives. A girl should keep herself clean, eat healthy foods and get proper exercise to remain in good physical condition, maintain her hair in an attractive style, and always present herself with an overall neat and well-manicured appearance.

Also, the law of kindness should be in her mouth. This principle addresses how she should treat others. When a young lady realizes that she is somebody because of who she is in Christ, her self-confidence will allow her to treat others with respect. She will possess the ability to regard others in the same manner that she herself expects to be treated.

Our self-concept is constantly evolving throughout our lives. However, no matter what may occur to damage our healthy sense of self, it will be restored when we hold fast to God's truth and power. The Word of God makes us realize that we are not our own; we have been bought with a price. This is the most important thing of all to know and convey to others. To have an understanding that God loves us so much that He made the ultimate sacrifice for us will shape our self-concept in a powerful way. We are precious to Him and honored in the sight of the Lord.

God can use everything that has happened to us to help mold us into the beautiful image of His Son. We are not who the world says we are, and we must not allow vain philosophies or contemporary culture to define us. Rather, we must purpose to embrace who God says we are and live as His image-bearers.

A considerable measure of our beauty and our self-concept come from knowing Christ. The sooner we get into the presence of our loving Father, who accepts and loves us unconditionally, the sooner we will be transformed and empowered to help transform the lives of others—even our own Black brothers and sisters.

REFERENCES

Anderson, N. 2006. *The Bondage Breaker®: Overcoming *Negative Thoughts *Irrational Feelings *Habitual Sins.* Eugene, Oregon: Harvest House.

Wilson, Sandra. 2001. *Hurt People Hurt People: Hope and Healing for Yourself and Your Relationships.* Grand Rapids: Discovery House.

SUGGESTED READINGS

Lee-Thorpe, K. and C. Hicks. 1997. *Why Beauty Matters.* Colorado Springs: NavPress.

McGee, R. S. 1998. *The Search for Significance.* Revised expanded edition. Nashville: Thomas Nelson Publishers.

Chapter Three

OUR PURPOSE:
A FIRST LADY'S
REVOLUTIONARY
CONVERSION

Karen Waddles

"*We'd really* like for you to come back and speak for us—as long as you don't speak on that topic." It was the mid-1990s at a church in the suburbs of Chicago. The pastor had requested that I hold classes at his church once a month for six months and the first topic was to be "The Role of Women in Ministry."

I passed out handouts to introduce the topic we would be discussing. This "make-believe" scenario was offered to get the discussion started:

Latrice had a dream last night. In her dream she was called to preach. She wakes up, overcome with excitement about her dream. She can even see herself pastoring her own church some day in the future. She can't wait to share the wonderful news with all of the members of the church. She is surprised at the mixed reactions she receives. Some say, "You go, girl! Let Him use you!" Others tell her to "stay in her place." Yet others encourage her to put her gifts to work within the women's ministry. How would you advise Latrice to handle this call? Can you support your answer with Scripture?

There was a strange heaviness in the air as the ladies looked at their handouts. They read this opening scenario and glanced back and forth at one another with wary looks. Finally, one of them said, "Why did you pick this topic to speak to us on?" Other questions followed quickly, "Who told you to do this?" "Do you know about the history of our church?" Clearly, this was going to be a very, very long day.

Whenever I have posed this same scenario to African American Christian women across the country, I typically receive the following mix of results:

I believe women can:

Preach and pastor	20 percent
Preach only	50 percent
Preach to/teach women only	10 percent
Unsure	20 percent

Furthermore, on the subject of the appropriate role for women in the ministry, there are two distinct views that are held within the church. For the purpose of our discussion, the following definitions will be helpful:

The **egalitarian** position is "a belief that since men and women share the image of God, and thus are equal in essence, no functional distinctions can be made between men and women" (House 1990, 14). Those persons who believe that women may preach and pastor would be described as egalitarians.

The **complementarian** position holds that women have virtual freedom of service in the church, except as elder or preacher/teacher of men. Those persons who believe that women can preach and teach (but only to women) would be categorized as complementarians.

What follows in this chapter is not a doctrinal treatise on the role of women in ministry; rather, I will present the truths that God has grafted into my heart. What I have discovered through study of God's Word has settled this issue for me. My earnest prayer is that once I have laid them out, these truths will do the same for you.

A PERSONAL STRUGGLE

In the early '70s, I was a part of the 20 percent crowd that believed strongly in egalitarian roles for women. Deeply impacted by the Black Power Movement, I was an afro- and dashiki-wearing sister of the Revolution. I sat at the altar of Angela Davis and Nikki Giovanni, two incredibly strong and radical Black women. I studied architectural engineering at the University of Kansas and was poised to enter a field that few Black women occupied at that time. At least, that's what I thought—but God had very different plans.

His plan was for me to marry a young man named George who would later be called to preach and pastor. But at that time I was still an afrocentric revolutionary with very distinct ideas about gender roles and what a sistah was or was not going to take. For the most part, George and I had much in common. We loved to talk, go to the movies, and play bid whist. However, his ideas about roles within marriage were diametrically opposed to mine. The idea of being a doting, submissive wife was archaic and distasteful to me. I had not seen that example growing up and had no desire to break the generational mold cast for me by the women in my life.

Nevertheless, prior to getting married, we decided that we would build our marriage and family based on the principles of the Bible. So, I went to God's Word to find support for my position. Surely, God didn't expect me to belittle my intelligence by submitting to a man! As I was confronted with the concepts of headship, submission, and biblical roles for marriage, I came to an awakening: a realization of how radically different God's ways and thoughts are than ours. They are so far beyond our capacity to understand that unless He reveals them to us, they cannot be known. My heart overflowed in appreciation for God's desire to make His will known to His children.

Along with this awakening came a sense of brokenness; the hardness that was part and parcel of my radical stance had to be reckoned with. It became clear to me that on the issue of submission my heart had to change. And it did—but not overnight. After agonizing in prayer for weeks and months with this new truth, I finally came to embrace His wisdom and to trust His plans for my life.

However, there were more questions to be answered than just those relating to marriage. If His will for women in marriage was submission to headship, what was His will for women in His church? I wondered, *Is it consistent with biblical principles to believe that God would intend for women to be submissive in marriage, on the one hand, yet have dominant roles in the church on the other hand? What are women who are as gifted and talented as men to do with their gifts in the church?*

The journey to discovery took me back again to God's Word and then to many books and resources on this topic. Some of them are listed at the conclusion of this chapter. For those who are interested in a more in-depth analysis, I invite you to consider each one thoughtfully and prayerfully.

Some Nonnegotiables

As we continue this sensitive and often controversial subject, a valid discussion must be built on the foundation of a few "nonnegotiables." When it comes to serving God, there are some things that we really need to agree on, whether we consider ourselves strongly entrenched in the egalitarian position or the complementarian position.

1. *God's Word is truth.* We cannot write off any portions of the Bible that may seem inconvenient because its teachings may appear chauvinistic or unsympathetic to women. The words of 2 Timothy 3:16 must resonate in the heart and mind of all believers: *"All Scripture is God-breathed and is useful for teaching, rebuking, correcting and training in righteousness."*

   We live in an age and time when truth is relative. However, this wasn't the case for our parents and grandparents. When I grew up in the 1950s and 1960s, there were some clear lines that were drawn between right and wrong. If you lied—that was wrong. If you lived a promiscuous lifestyle—that was wrong. If you took things that didn't belong to you—that was wrong. But today the lines have all shifted. If they exist at all, they are virtual lines that adjust to accommodate one's changing fancies.

But there is one thing that is unchanging, and I rejoice in that! With the shifting sands of our culture and everyone doing *"what is right in their own eyes"* (see Judges 17:6b) it is so comforting to know that God's truth is *the* Truth—and it never changes. It's not impacted by the laws we pass, or the presidents we elect, or by any movement. I came to the realization that nothing supersedes the Word of Truth, whether it's the Black Power movement, the feminist movement, or any other movement. God has breathed out His will through His Word and it is what I need to live right, to believe right, and to develop spiritual maturity.

2. *God has a tender heart for women and sees them as equal in worth to men.* During His ministry, Jesus was radical in His response to women. He went against virtually every convention and expectation of the Jewish system of His day. He allowed and encouraged women to be taught (Luke 10:38–42). He spoke with a Samaritan woman in a public place and taught her spiritual truth (John 4:4–42). He allowed a woman to touch Him in public (Mark 14:3–6), and He defended a woman of ill repute (John 8:7). Throughout His ministry, Jesus interacted and discoursed with women in a way that forever elevated their status.

   However, there is a direct contrast to Jesus' actions that placed women in a cherished and loftier place. Although He was willing to go against the culture of His day, Jesus chose not to appoint women as apostles. There are Scripture passages that speak specifically to the issue of women's roles that make it easy to come away from them wondering whether God sees women almost as second-class citizens.

When I approached these controversial portions of Scripture from an egalitarian point of view, one of the verses that really connected with me in my support for equal roles in the church was Galatians 3:28. In this verse, Paul asserts that *"There is neither Jew nor Greek, slave nor free, male nor female, for you are all one in Christ Jesus."* That was just what I was looking for! Clearly God was saying that there are no distinctions between men and women once we become believers! I was now armed—and truly dangerous.

Upon further review, other Scriptures on this topic seemed to contradict my first impression. So, I went back to Galatians 3:28 and read it again. This time I took its entire context into consideration. It was evident after an examination of the whole chapter that biblical roles had nothing to do with the text. The author was not arguing that role distinctions were erased at Calvary. If that were so, then those who were slaves would have been emancipated as soon as they accepted Christ as Savior (*"there is neither slave nor free"*). These distinctions remained even after receiving Christ.

My study of Galatians, chapter 3 revealed that Paul was challenging the Galatian believers because they had returned to a salvation based on works. He makes the point that all believers are justified by faith—and faith alone. This truth applies to everyone who believes in Christ Jesus, whether Jew or Greek, male or female, slave or free. Paul argues that regardless of one's nationality, status, or gender, every believer stands on equal footing in Christ. There are no second-class citizens in God's family.

I concluded that, rather than giving license and permission for women to preach or pastor, instead Galatians 3:28 affirms the worth of every woman: God sees us with equal standing and equal worth with our male counterparts.

3. *There is only one truth.* If my position and/or experience are not consonant with Scripture, then I must be in error. As a result, I am challenged to ask God to open my eyes to His truth.

If two mutually exclusive points are made, both cannot possibly be true. In the words of Romans 3:4, *"Let God be true, and every man a liar."* Many of us may have female family members or friends who are preaching or possibly pastoring. Maybe you have announced your personal call to preach. Most women who exercise their gifts in this way have a deep, abiding love for the Lord. Their earnest desire is to serve Him well. This is not a personal attack on any of those persons. This is an effort to elevate Scripture above personal experience and allow God's Word to reign supreme.

As I make this point in teaching sessions, often a woman will challenge, "But Deborah was a judge. That proves that God doesn't have a problem with women preaching or pastoring!" I thank her and proceed to address this assertion. If Deborah was the first of a long line of female judges who exercised leadership in the Old Testament, this might be a strong argument. But, she was very much the exception. Deborah fulfilled her role of judge in a very different manner than all of the male judges. Moreover, her role was not a public one but more one-on-one consultation. She did not lead the army of Israel into battle as the other judges did. And there is every indication that she judged during a time in Israel's history when men were weak.

Barak seems to have been God's choice (Judges 4), yet even after Deborah informed him of God's desire for him to lead the children of Israel in battle (which was a function of judges), he demonstrated his weakness by insisting that she accompany him. If anything, this account in Judges demonstrates what happens when men shirk their responsibilities and calling. This says to me that in a vacuum God will use another vessel.

Others may say, "What can we do if there aren't any men in our church who are capable of teaching?" Many churches that have wrestled with God's truths regarding gender roles have faced this same dilemma. Our church was like that when we arrived twenty-five years ago. There were mixed classes (both men and women) that were being taught by women. The women were good teachers, but we were concerned that they were out of place teaching men. We began to pray fervently, asking God to send us men who were apt to teach, who had a heart for the Word.

You can guess what happened, right? God honored His Word. He sent faithful men who were on fire for the Word of God. And the most wonderful fringe benefit occurred for the church. Role models emerged and young boys were able to see godly men as teachers and true leaders in the church.

In other situations, women have said, "If my pastor approves of me serving in a copastor role and teaching men, is that okay?" This is, perhaps, the most difficult question to address, because I have great respect for pastors as the authority in the church. However, it is difficult to argue that anyone, even a pastor, can give permission for a woman to do something that God's Word clearly forbids.

After it's all said and done, there is usually someone who still says, "I don't care what you say, I *know* that the Lord spoke directly to me and told me to preach His Word." It's really hard to argue with anyone's personal experience. I can't know what any individual's experience has been. I can only know what His Word says. I also know that His will never does battle with His Word. To those women, I ask only that they hear from their hearts what the Word says.

GOD'S WORD FOR OUR ISSUE

As women of God, we must first recognize that God is a God of order. And there is a defined structure that supports how He established His church

to be run. The apostle Paul said it best when he addressed the church: *"Let all things be done decently and in order"* (1 Corinthians 14:40 KJV).

May I summarize for you the key verses that settled in my heart the issue of a woman's rightful place in the ministry? I highly recommend that you turn to the Bible and read them within their entire context. I must admit that you may find their message pretty difficult to swallow. They might even make you want to turn away. But, please don't do that. Please stay with me so we can make this journey of realization together.

Through much study and research, I have discovered that the Bible supports the complementarian position for women who desire to answer the call to ministry. Yes, women have a critical place in God's ministry plans. We can and need to serve in the church. However, we are to do so in accordance with God's will for us. The Word of God explains His will. Therefore, when we know His Word, we also know His will. Then we must follow Jesus' example: when praying to the Father, He affirmed, *"Your word is truth"* (John 17:17).

> *Your desire will be for your husband, and he will rule over you.*
> (Genesis 3:16)

At first blush and in its literal context, this verse applies to marriage. However, in the broader context, it also helps to explain our problem with biblical roles. This one verse helped me to finally come to terms with why the topic of submission to male leadership is so hard to accept. When God speaks to Eve after sin has been brought into the world, He pronounces the effects sin will have on women in this life.

The first consequence is something to which nearly every woman who has borne a child can attest: pain in childbirth. The second consequence is what opened my eyes in my struggle to prove my former egalitarian position. When she invited her husband to participate in an act of disobedience to God, Eve had chosen to leave her place of submission and *lead* Adam rather than *follow* him. From that moment forward, every woman and girl would struggle with an inner compulsion to do the same thing. The word *desire* means "to take over" or "to rule."

This impulse applies to more than just the situation of marriage. On any playground in America, there can be six children playing, and if at least one of them is a girl, more than likely she will be calling the shots and directing the activity. You see, as females, we have this internal "management gene" that we must work to keep under control wherever we happen to be: in the home, in the church, and yes, even on the playground.

Sin has such a damaging effect on God's divine order. The latter half of Genesis 3:16 suggests that men will behave in an overbearing or chauvinistic (*"and he will rule over you"*) manner. God's original intent was for women to submit and for men to lead lovingly. But since sin entered the equation, we must all struggle to control the effect of original sin. It has the power to summon the tendency in us as women to dominate men. And it conjures up the tendency in men to be domineering and overly aggressive or, conversely, weak and silent as Adam was. Thank God we have the Holy Spirit to help us overcome the temptation to give in to our flesh. He has given us the ability to combat the urges to step outside of our God-given roles.

> *Now I want you to realize that the head of every man is Christ, and the head of the woman is man, and the head of Christ is God.* (1 Corinthians 11:3)

It's important to note where this verse refers to the word "head" Paul used the word *kephale,* which means "governing, ruling organ." And the last portion of this verse speaks so powerfully: "the head of Christ is God." It is where we are to focus if we want to understand the order Paul is laying out here. If God the Father and God the Son are equal in essence—and they are—then Christ submitted Himself to God the Father to accomplish the work of redemption.

So submission is not a matter of essence or superiority because, even though He submitted to the Father, Christ was still equal with God. Furthermore, they are on the same level in terms of Deity so there is no question of superiority. When Christ as the Son of God submitted to God the Father, it had to do with role and function. Therefore, we can conclude that roles and functions do not have to be identical to prove that the parties are equal in essence. When we understand this principle, this helps us as women to deal with the feeling of being inferior or less competent than men that is deeply rooted in the issue of submission.

In reality, we deal with this in practical ways every day. For example, when the crossing guard at the corner holds up his hand for us to stop, we don't question whether he has the right to do so, or whether he's more or less educated than we are. We submit to his authority in order to get safely across the street. When the flight attendant on the airplane says that the seat belts need to be fastened and seats placed in the upright position before the plane takes off, we don't question whether he has a right to tell us what to do. If we want to fly, we submit.

So, the question becomes, if we can submit to the flight attendant and the crossing guard without question, then why won't we submit to the male leadership God mandates for His church without charging God with sexism and chauvinism?

> *A woman should learn in quietness and full submission. I do not permit a woman to teach or to have authority over a man; she must be silent. For Adam was formed first, then Eve.* (1 Timothy 2:11–13)

The apostle Paul wrote to Timothy, his son in the ministry, to encourage him and provide clear instructions for the oversight of the church at Ephesus. Paul was concerned that false teaching had invaded the church. A key part of his instruction is directed at how women should behave within the congregation of believers. These directives apply when the setting is mixed—both men and women were present. He argues that women should have an attitude of submission and quietness. Women are not to do so because we are of lesser value, or because we don't have much to offer; rather, it is because of divine order. It was God's choice to create man first. When God made the decision to create Adam first, it indicated that He designed man's role to be that of headship and leadership.

Does that mean women have to be completely silent? Of course not! Women have full authority to teach women, but when it comes to the teaching of men—we are to be silent. I would argue that this "silence" carries with it the idea that we are to have a "softness" about us that says, "I am a woman. I am not trying to be a man in a female body. I understand the uniqueness God gave me and I relish it."

Can I say it like this? I think that would mean that if a woman is reading the Scripture or praying in a worship service, there should be a distinctly feminine manner in which she carries this out. She should not be whooping and hollering like a man! This biblical term for silence is *hesuchia,* which carries with it the idea that the woman has a quiet control from within and it is demonstrated in how she carries herself. She is not loud and out of control. An easy-to-remember rule of thumb is this: *A woman never demands or commands, she always asks and appeals.*

Recently, I encountered a good example of how women should not behave. My husband and I stopped at a rib joint after attending a worship service across town. It was a hopping place on the South Side of Chicago. There was a long line of people waiting to get their hands on some of the best ribs in town. Inside, behind the counter were five men and one woman cooking up those incredible-tasting ribs.

Obviously, the woman was in charge. She was barking orders left and right, "Where's that order of rib tips? Put that over there! Didn't I *tell* you to . . . ?" And all of this was at a volume that was a few decibels higher than necessary, with a tone that was completely inappropriate. And the men? They just took it. They continued to do their work and none of them crossed words with her. But they all wore the same look on their faces. It was the look of shame and humiliation.

There is something truly emasculating about a group of men being ordered around by a loud woman, even in the secular realm. It just doesn't seem right. It *feels* out of order. And, guess what? It *is* out of order. That not only goes for the secular realm and the home—but also in the church.

> *Here is a trustworthy saying: If anyone sets his heart on being an overseer, he desires a noble task. Now the overseer must be above reproach, the husband of but one wife, temperate, self-controlled, respectable, hospitable, able to teach, not given to drunkenness, not violent but gentle, not quarrelsome, not a lover of money.* (1 Timothy 3:1–3)

Paul continues in this same letter to Timothy. In the next chapter, he clarifies the qualifications for a pastor. He makes it clear that a pastor must be the "husband of but one wife." It goes without saying that it is impossible for a woman to fulfill this qualification. If Scripture does not permit a woman to teach or lead men, it stands to reason that a woman would not be allowed to pastor them.

There are different kinds of gifts, but the same Spirit. There are different kinds of service, but the same Lord. There are different kinds of working, but the same God works all of them in all men. (1 Corinthians 12:4–6)

This passage from 1 Corinthians, chapter 12 makes it clear that God distributes spiritual gifts without respect of persons. He gives some the gifts of preaching, teaching, and/or pastoring (shepherding) and there is no indication that these gifts are gender specific. Herein lies the problem. I believe that many women are well-intentioned and are gifted to teach, preach, and even pastor, but many of us have not consulted the whole of Scripture to learn His intent for how those gifts are to be used.

Here is where the feminist argument really digs in and does the greatest damage. It feeds on the vulnerability of women who want with all their hearts to serve God and use their gifts to His glory. Some of the verses we've considered, as well as others, make it clear that there are specific offices and roles that God has designated for men only.

Satan has done his best to fan the flames of discontent in the hearts of women and the yield has been a feeling that we are second-class citizens. He has deceived many women into thinking that unless we can do everything that men can do, we will not be satisfied. But, God has a chosen work for each one of us who has a heart to serve Him and His people—and whatever it may be for you, know that it is in accordance with His Word.

Ministry Unfettered

What does a woman who is gifted to speak, preach, and pastor do with her gifts? How can her gifts be best used to God's glory and in keeping with His Word?

The book of Titus, chapter 2 provides a wonderful model of how God intends for the church to function. It's an organizational chart in many ways. Paul provides instruction to another young pastor, Titus, on how to organize the church to fulfill its ministry in Crete. Unmistakably, the pastor occupies the top level of the organizational chart. He is the primary preacher, teacher, and exhorter.

The second level of the organizational chart is quite intriguing as Paul addresses various groups within the church and instructs Titus to teach the older men to have qualities that reflect the fruit of the Spirit (2:1–2); rebuke the younger men and exhort them to have good character (2:6); and finally, he tells Titus to teach the older (mature) women how to behave (2:3).

There is, however, a group that is conspicuously absent from this second tier of church organization. The younger women are the only group that falls to the third tier. Moreover, they are strategically placed under the tutelage of the mature women. Paul encourages Titus to entrust the care, teaching, and shepherding of young women to the mature women (2:3–5). I believe with all my heart that this is the place God has set aside specifically for women who have a shepherd's heart and a desire to teach His truth. There is an abundant wealth of knowledge and experience that mature women can share and use to encourage young women to have a closer walk with Christ.

With the older women being told to "*train the younger women to love their husbands and children, to be self-controlled and pure, to be busy at home, to be kind, and to be subject to their husbands, so that no one will malign the word of God*" (Titus 2:4–5), can there be any more appropriate and desperately needed message than this for Christian women today?

Television shows like *Wife Swap* and *Nanny 911* provide a telling look into homes across America. Children are being raised with little or no parental supervision, no regard for sexual morals, and little or no respect for their parents. The sad truth is that many women have taken leave of our primary responsibility to take care of the home, and out of this neglect has come every manner of evil that one can imagine.

But, God is calling us back to this work. Women need to be pastored by women. Women need to be shepherded by women. The example of Ruth and Naomi is a picture of the tender nature of the shepherding relationship between the mature woman and the younger woman. Through this loving instruction, can you hear the tenderness in Naomi's voice as she teaches Ruth how to respond to Boaz: "*One day Naomi her mother-in-law said to her, 'My daughter, should I not try to find a home for you, where you will be well provided for? Is not Boaz, with whose servant girls you have been, a kinsman of ours? Tonight he will be winnowing barley on the threshing floor. Wash and perfume yourself, and put on your best clothes. Then go down to the threshing floor, but don't let him know you are there until he has finished eating and drinking*'" (Ruth 3:1–3).

Boaz was a good man who chose to honor Ruth. This is how he responded to the way in which she approached him: *"And now, my daughter, don't be afraid. I will do for you all you ask. All my fellow townsmen know that you are a woman of noble character"* (Ruth 3:11). The end result of their exchange was that Boaz married Ruth. And to this union was born Obed, the father of Jesse, who was the father of King David, an ancestor of Jesus Christ. Imagine what may have happened to Ruth if she had not had the benefit of godly counsel, teaching, and shepherding from Naomi. She could have become a victim, rather than the victorious woman who figured into the lineage of Christ.

Let's be honest, ladies. There are few churches in the African American culture that are not *overwhelmingly* populated by women. There are churches filled with women like Ruth who desperately need the heart, the touch, the shepherding of a godly woman. How many of them have fallen through the cracks because we were busy in pursuit of a calling that was not ours? The potential for real ministry is huge. Could it be that we have neglected this primary call in pursuit of a different "call" that God is not even calling us to?

It's Personal . . . Embracing His Truth

How do you handle truth that challenges your reality? Do you reject it? Do you back away and take some time to adjust to it? Or do you embrace it? I understand all of those responses, for they were mine at different times along my journey. To be quite honest, I was afraid of these truths. When I began to earnestly study the role of women in ministry, I was speaking at a good number of churches for women's day services. The congregation was always mixed with men and women. And I liked how things were.

God's Word meant more than life to me, but the fears were real too. How would people respond to me? Would they attack and ostracize me because of this change of heart? What if I never got another invitation to speak again?

I felt a palpable tugging on my heart to take a stand, to make this truth the reality for my life and practice. For me, that meant I must decline invitations to speak to mixed groups. At first it was really awkward. The women's day chairperson would call and I'd say, "I'm sorry but I won't be able to do that." The temptation was always great to excuse myself because of a schedule conflict, but that is often not the case; it would mean that I'd be lying. Then, when I say, "my position on the role of women in ministry prevents me from speaking to mixed groups," there is always an awkward silence. With one exception of a lady who hung up the phone very abruptly, for the most part, there is a polite good-bye before the conversation ends.

On the other hand, God has faithfully provided me with incredible opportunities for ministry exclusively to women. One-on-one counseling opportunities abound, and there is no scarcity of women's conferences, retreats, prayer breakfasts, and so on to exercise every spiritual gift.

This issue was the topic of a class at a national convention in Memphis for an entire week. As we came to the close of the last session, a middle-aged woman raised her hand. With tears in her eyes, she stood to speak. She said, "I never understood why I never felt quite right standing in my husband's pulpit and preaching on Sundays. And, I now understand why God has been sending one woman after the other to me for counseling. That's my calling!" She was radiant and the heart peace she was experiencing was very visible.

If you have been struggling with a similar experience in your life, how does God desire for you to respond to these truths? Is He looking for a change in the way that you view ministry? Are you afraid of making a radical change? If so, I understand that, and so does God. But, as you discover truth, I hope you will be faithful to follow His Word in obedience, however it may lead you.

More Ministry Opportunities

You should know that the sky is the limit for ministry opportunities for women that fit well into the parameters of biblical principles. Any role with the exception of pastoring or teaching men is appropriate. For more on this topic, I highly recommend that you read the book *Recovering Biblical Manhood and Womanhood: A Response to Evangelical Feminism*, by Wayne Grudem and John Piper (1991).

I would strongly highlight the need for women to use their shepherding gifts in the area of counseling other women. A great resource that relates specifically to this topic is *The Role of Women in Ministry: Affirming the Biblical Position of Women in the Church* by H. Wayne House (1990). Author H. Wayne House summarizes the biblical principle of utilizing the gifts and calling of women in the church: "Suffice it to say that the pastoral staff that fails to draw on the biblical resource of qualified older women in the congregation is not only risking the effectiveness of its ministry, it is operating in clear contradiction to the instruction of Titus 2:4–5" (House 1990, 189). This book closes with wonderful recommendations in regard to women's gifts and their vital importance in ministry.

Ministry to youth also offers a broad range of possibilities. Can you envision conferences and retreats at churches across the nation where women are teaching young girls about sexual purity and the joys of saving themselves until marriage? What if these retreats or conferences launched a program of study in the area of purity, encompassing topics on intimacy with God, positive self-image, fundamentals of dating, and preparing for marriage?

Could you see these experiences culminating with formal ceremonies where the girls and boys make a purity pledge to God and their future spouses? These ceremonies could be something very simple or something as elaborate as a cotillion/botillion. Such possibilities provide the opportunity for women to bring all of their gifts to bear in a way that shapes and changes young lives for eternity!

And what about writing? Writing is simply the spoken word, put onto paper. African Americans are voracious readers! We love books! There is a famine in the land for African American writers who can write fiction and tell powerful stories against the backdrop of Christian principles. What better way to reach a postmodern culture than through the power of story with a message? Maybe that urge you have to "say it" is a prompting to write it.

CONCLUSION

As for me, I guess you could say that this "would-be revolutionary" has come a long way. I still maintain that women are every bit as insightful and intelligent as men. We are. We have to be in order to get our heads around this truth, embrace it, and beat back that part of us that still wants to reject it.

And, as for that church in the Chicago suburbs? It has been over a decade and I never went back. It was clear that the ladies were ready to do battle around this issue, and that would not have honored Christ in any way. I think that's a good reminder for us as we close this conversation. We bring great reproach on the name of our Lord when we fight or argue about this issue.

If you have been angered by what you've read, I encourage you to acknowledge that anger and let it work the good that God has purposed in your life. Take some time to meditate on what I have shared and what has perhaps agitated or caused you some consternation. Please take whatever the Holy Spirit reveals to you before the Lord and be open to what God has to say to you about your concerns and your purpose in Him. Consider your options of response as God ministers to you and be faithful to act upon His truth.

I pray, my sisters, that we will all continue to remain faithful to the truth we know, until we meet Him—the only real Truth—face-to-face.

REFERENCES

House, H. Wayne. 1990. *The Role of Women in Ministry Today: Affirming the Biblical Position of Women in the Church.* Nashville: Thomas Nelson.

Piper, John, and Wayne Grudem. 1991. *Recovering Biblical Manhood and Womanhood: A Response to Evangelical Feminism.* Wheaton: Crossway Books.

SUGGESTED READINGS

Carter, Norvel, and Matthew Parker. 1996. *Woman to Woman: Perspectives of Fifteen African American Christian Women.* Grand Rapids: Zondervan.

Easley, Cindy. 2008. *What's Submission Got to Do with It? Find Out from a Woman Like You.* Chicago: Moody Publishers.

McCulley, Carolyn. 2008. *Radical Womanhood: Feminine Faith in a Feminist World.* Chicago: Moody Publishers.

Saucy, Robert, and Judith TenElshof. 2001. *Women and Men in Ministry: A Complementary Perspective.* Chicago: Moody Publishers.

Chapter Four

IN PURSUIT OF
A HEALTHY LIFESTYLE

*Do you not know that your body is
a temple of the Holy Spirit, who is in you,
whom you have received from God? You are not
your own; you were bought at a price.
Therefore honor God with your body.*

I CORINTHIANS 6:19–20

Dr. Taffy Anderson

The Obesity Problem

There is a major epidemic going on within the Black population that Black Americans, particularly Black women, tend to ignore. Despite all of the challenges we face in this country, adult and childhood obesity is one of the fastest growing health problems in the United States. In fact, 76 percent of Black adults are overweight or obese and approximately 45 percent are obese. In 2001, the Surgeon General published a report stating that obesity and the number of overweight people had reached epidemic proportions in the United States.

Looking strictly at Black women, the statistics are alarming. By gender and race, this demographic is the leading group affected by the obesity problem, with a shocking 81.6 percent of Black women being overweight or obese and 53.9 percent suffering from obesity. As such, obesity is a major health issue that needs to be addressed because of all the health implications that are associated with this condition.

I am a medical doctor who also happens to be a Black woman. One of my deepest passions is for people, particularly my Black sisters, to have knowledge that will empower them to live healthy lives. But first we must understand that enjoying the blessing of a healthy life is contingent on doing the right things to keep our bodies in good shape—physically and spiritually. To that end, please allow me to give you some important and practical information that you can apply to prevent you from becoming overweight or obese.

If you happen to already be in these categories, there is still some good news for you. With some knowledge about what to do and what not to do, you can do much to reverse your situation. I also ask that you pass on the following information to your friends and loved ones. Perhaps you have children of your own or children touch your life in some way or another. You can help future generations by educating them about how to prevent obesity. It will be a great blessing to you and a valuable gift that they will cherish throughout their lives.

WHAT IS OBESITY?

More than women in any other race, Black women have some very serious health challenges that stem from obesity. Obesity is now defined as a chronic health condition or disease that is characterized by excess adipose tissue. Adipose cells are fat cells in the body that store fat.

Obesity is measured as weight in kilograms divided by height in meters squared (kg/m^2). This is called your *body mass index* (BMI). It sounds complicated but you need to be aware of your proximity to being obese. But you don't have to figure it out; there are several websites that will calculate it for you. Go to the National Heart, Lung and Blood Institute's website at www.nhlbi.nih.gov, enter BMI in the search column and the BMI page will appear. Type in your height in inches and weight in pounds and it will calculate your BMI.

See the table below for the definitions of BMI. If you are in the overweight category, you will have a BMI greater than or equal to 25. Obesity is defined as a BMI greater than or equal to 30. If you are not in the normal range, make a note of the normal range (18.5–24.9) and use it as a long-term goal for you to meet.

TABLE 1. CLASSIFICATION OF OVERWEIGHT AND OBESITY BY BMI

Underweight	BMI < 18.5
Normal weight	BMI 18.5–24.9
Overweight	BMI 25–29.9
Obese	BMI 30–39.9
Morbid obesity	BMI 40 or greater

The Complications of Obesity

Being obese is not just an issue of physical appearance; it has the insidious potential to create havoc in one's life. You may be surprised to find that there are numerous health problems linked to having an obesity condition. It increases the risk of type 2 diabetes, hypertension, heart disease, elevated cholesterol, and stroke. As if that weren't enough, being obese also increases the risk of cancer of the uterus, postmenopausal breast cancer, and cancer of the colon and rectum. In addition, obesity complications have been linked to osteoarthritis, liver, and gallbladder disease, as well as sleep apnea. Furthermore, obesity can cause menstrual irregularities, urinary incontinence, and infertility problems.

Now let's look at some of these diseases that represent major issues for Black women. You will notice that reducing your weight is a recurring key to avoiding the risk of having these diseases. Keep this in mind; it is worth starting a safe exercise regimen. It could make the difference in combating against the onset of a myriad of problems.

Type 2 Diabetes

Type 2 diabetes is the most common type of diabetes seen in adults. It is a condition in which the body has elevated blood sugars. One of the major risks for developing type 2 diabetes is being overweight. Diabetes is more prevalent in Black women than in White women; one in four Black women over the age of fifty-five has diabetes. Some of the complications from diabetes include blindness, kidney disease, and cardiovascular disease, which can lead to heart attacks. But, you should know that decreasing your weight can reduce your risk for diabetes. We will later discuss some ways to do just that.

Hypertension

Hypertension is called high blood pressure. It is defined as a blood pressure greater than or equal to 140/90. Black women have the highest rates of high blood pressure among all U.S. women. Approximately 37 percent of Black women in the United States have high blood pressure.[3] We tend to develop hypertension at an earlier age than White women and are more likely to suffer from the complications of elevated blood pressure. Some of the major complications of high blood pressure include heart disease, kidney disease, and stroke. However, it is known that weight loss can demonstrate an improvement in blood pressure.

Heart Disease and Stroke

Heart disease is the number one killer of both men and women. However, it is more prevalent in Black women than White women. Black women also have a greater risk of death from heart disease than women of other races.

Stroke is the third leading cause of death for Black women, with cancer being the second. Research studies have shown that being overweight, obese, and having excess abdominal fat can increase a person's risk for elevated triglycerides and cholesterol. These substances deposit in the arteries of the heart and other blood vessels and cause narrowing of the arteries that can lead to heart attacks and strokes. It is known that a decrease in weight will reduce your risk for heart disease and possible strokes.

Osteoarthritis

Osteoarthritis is a joint disease in which the cartilages of the joints wear away. Being overweight or obese puts excess weight and tension on the joints, causing them to wear down. When a woman is overweight, it may also cause inflammatory substances to be released from fat cells that can lead to further damage to the joints. However, losing excess weight can decrease the risk for developing this disease by taking the stress off the bones and cartilage.

Cancers Linked to Obesity

Several forms of cancer are attributed to obesity in women. Endometrial cancer is the most common cancer of the uterus and obese women have a two to four times greater risk of developing this form of cancer than those at a normal weight. Although endometrial cancer is more common among White women, Black women who develop the disease are more likely to present in later stages of the disease and subsequently die from the disease.

Breast cancer is more common among White women than Black women; however, Black women are more likely to present in later stages of the disease and are two times more likely than Whites to die from this disease. According to research studies, postmenopausal breast cancer has been linked to women who are overweight and obese.

Colorectal cancer is one of the leading cancers in Black women. According to the American Cancer Society, Black women are more likely to die from colorectal cancer than any other racial or ethnic group.

Altogether, we have touched on some major diseases that affect Black women in particular. Once again, research has shown that a woman can reduce her risk of developing these cancers if she loses weight and maintains the weight loss.

Other diseases that are associated with being overweight or obese are: elevated cholesterol, fatty liver, gallbladder disease, and sleep apnea.

Ladies, at the risk of sounding redundant—the bottom line is—it's important to lose weight. That is because the diseases I have discussed here could be prevented if we maintain a proper weight. The illnesses associated with obesity are far too serious and we must not take this subject lightly. But, be encouraged, even just a small reduction in weight can lower your chances of getting them and increase your chances of staying healthy.

WHAT CAUSES OBESITY?

By now, I hope that I have captured your attention. You are probably wondering what causes obesity in the first place and how we can avoid it. There are several reasons why people are overweight or obese; some of them include: advancing age, gender, and genetic makeup. In addition to these factors, eating habits, physical activity, psychological factors, medical illnesses, and certain medications can lead a person to gain weight. Let's explore some of these causes in more detail.

1) As we age, the body's metabolism slows down and we have a tendency to gain weight. Women have a lower rate of metabolism than men, which predisposes us to weight gain. After menopause, the metabolic rate decreases even further and contributes to the weight gain that is so commonly seen in the postmenopausal years.

2) One of the major causes of being overweight or obese is a person's eating habits. I know that this is a sensitive subject because it poses a challenge to the practices we have developed over the course of our lives. The truth is, the body needs a certain amount of energy to maintain its daily function and that energy is derived from the foods we eat. If we overeat, then the extra

energy is stored as fat. That fat ultimately leads to weight gain.

Overeating is not uncommon in the African American culture and it is often a learned behavior. On Sunday afternoon, it would not be unusual to find fried chicken, collard greens, sweet potatoes, and corn bread on our plates. Overeating may be encouraged during these times and we must be careful to limit our portions (as well as those of our children).

Eating foods high in calories and saturated fats like those found at fast-food restaurants can cause us to gain weight. The "biggie size" portions offered at these eating establishments are way above the standard portions recommended; in fact, they can be considered unhealthy portions.

The healthy approach is to adhere to the standard portion sizes, stay away from the high calories and saturated fats, and increase your fruit and vegetable intake to five servings per day as recommended. Directing your eating habits in this way would start you well on your way to healthier living.

3) A lack of exercise is another primary reason we are overweight. Black women compared to White women exercise less and are more sedentary. Could it be because as a culture we have not been encouraged to exercise? Studies have shown time after time that those who live a sedentary lifestyle have increased their chances of becoming obese and overweight. It has been shown that exercise can reduce your risk for type 2 diabetes, heart disease, hypertension, the cancers already discussed, as well as pain from arthritis.

4) Research has shown that if the child's parents are obese, then the child has an increased risk of obesity. Researchers have found that there is evidence of a genetic cause for obesity and it might be related to a gene or groups of genes that cause a person to gain weight or develop more fat cells than the average person. But rest assured, researchers have also concluded that this is probably not a major cause of obesity. With the help of wise food choices and exercise, a person who might have hereditary predisposition to gain weight can achieve a normal weight. So we are not off the hook here, ladies!

5) Psychological factors such as stress and depression can cause weight gain in Black women. Unfortunately, in this fast-paced culture that we live in, we have a tendency to underestimate the amount of stress in our lives. To address the demands of the multiple roles that we play, women have become quite adept at multitasking. Depending on our individual circumstances, there are various situations we find ourselves in that contribute to the pressures of

life: for example, maintaining a godly marital relationship, managing careers, living in singlehood, raising children by ourselves because of absentee fathers, dealing with finances, and taking care of our elderly parents (just to name a few).

Furthermore, sometimes we are exposed to many of these situations at the same time and don't realize we are coping with incredible amounts of stress. Symptoms that result from these kinds of experiences include: mood swings, anger episodes, restlessness, fatigue, and the feeling of being anxious all the time. One of the body's responses to stress is an increase in cortisol, which is a hormone that can cause a woman to gain weight in the abdominal area. During stressful times, it is much harder to lose the weight because this hormone may be elevated and working against your efforts to lose weight.

Depression can alter your eating habits, leading to either weight gain or weight loss. In some women, depression can cause weight gain secondary to mood changes leading them to consume unhealthy foods and increasing the amount of foods they eat. In other women, depression can cause an unhealthy weight loss by a lack of appetite; but, in either case, depression should be taken seriously and evaluated by a health professional.

6) Certain medical diseases can cause a person to become overweight, such as Cushing's syndrome and hypothyroid disease. In addition, some medications like steroid hormones can cause an individual to gain weight. In the cases of medical diseases and medications, it is not a woman's doing that causes her to gain weight; however, she should take certain measures to alter her eating habits and try including exercise to offset the weight gain.

THE SPIRITUAL ASPECT OF OBESITY

Now that we have discussed the physical causes of being overweight, let's consider what is happening in the spiritual realm. What does God think about us being overweight and obese? Does the Bible have anything to say about being overweight? In Jesus' time, it is said that people walked approximately twenty miles per day. The women were in charge of the daily chores—getting water, gathering and preparing food. To accomplish their tasks, they may have traveled several miles to find both. Since fulfilling their duties involved strenuous exercise, obesity was probably not a major problem for them.

Today, women also play many roles in life; we are Christians who love the Lord and serve Him in various capacities, wives, mothers, career women, and so on. Since God has entrusted us with many gifts and talents, it stands to reason that He would have us to live healthy lives so that we can effectively carry out our duties and responsibilities. Taking care of our physical bodies is just one more thing that we need to attend to. This is all a part of fulfilling God's will as it relates to us. Our response to God should be to first obey Him in taking up the tasks with which He blesses us and then to approach those tasks with reverence and deference to His will.

Although the Bible may not mention being overweight directly, it does address the importance of taking care of our bodies. The apostle Paul addressed the Corinthian church concerning the reverence they should have for their bodies because they belonged to God. He asked them, *"Do you not know that your body is a temple of the Holy Spirit, who is in you, whom you have received from God?"* (1 Corinthians 6:19). Here Paul was talking to a group of believers who were recently saved but were still sleeping with temple prostitutes, which was a pagan religious custom of that day. He tells them that they should flee such sexual immorality because it is a sin against God.

Paul had to remind them that they now belonged to Jesus Christ and they should *not* defile their bodies by uniting themselves with prostitutes. He continued to correct them by saying, *"You are not your own; you were bought with a price. Therefore honor God with your body"* (1 Corinthians 6:19–20). The man of God explained to them that whoever slept with a prostitute was, in effect, also uniting Christ with a prostitute. What a horrible, degrading thought! But, he needed to make them understand the spiritual reality that was taking place when they indulged their bodies in sin.

If we follow Paul's teaching, we can conclude that God does care what we do in these bodies. Therefore, we too should flee sexual immorality because we are not our own. Our bodies are the temple of the Holy Spirit and we must honor God because we belong to Him. In regard to obesity and being overweight, this means we should stay as healthy as we can by eating the right foods in the proper portions, exercising regularly, and keeping our stress levels down. These practices are a good routine that will enable us to live healthier lives for the time God has given us on this earth to carry out His will.

But how do we accomplish this? It's not that any woman wants to be overweight or obese and that we wouldn't give anything to lose weight, right? Then how do we begin to lose weight so that we can honor God with our bodies? As Christian women, the answer lies in totally surrendering our lives over to God.

ALL TO THEE, I SURRENDER . . .

Now, we know that God is concerned about what we do in our bodies and wants us to honor Him. Then, what must we do? In Romans 12:1, the apostle Paul says to us: *"offer your bodies as living sacrifices, holy and pleasing to God— this is your spiritual act of worship."* The King James Version refers to this act of surrender as "your reasonable service." So it is about **surrender.** God has bought us with the blood of Jesus Christ and He wants us to surrender our mind, body, and soul to be used by Him.

Although we have a free will and the right to make our own decisions, God is asking us to make a conscious decision to surrender our lives to Him. In this verse, Paul is making the case that surrendering our decisions, rights, and will over to God should be our response because of all that God has done for us. We should want Him to make decisions for us because we love Him and He knows what is best for us.

I read about a good example of this recently. In his daily devotional, Watchman Nee tells about a Christian brother who was taking a train ride. When he was asked by some strangers to play cards, he told them that he could not because he did not bring his hands with him. He explained that because he was a Christian his hands did not belong to him but to God. He did not feel that playing cards was something that would honor God. Though he could have made his own decision to play cards, he made a conscious decision to surrender his will to the will of God and, consequently, said no.

In other words, when it comes to how we take care of our bodies, we can take a similar approach in surrendering our will to God. Many foods are high in calories and fats, so we should refrain from eating them because we know that they would make us unhealthy by causing us to gain weight, increase our cholesterol, and subject us to obesity-related diseases. And, none of that would bring honor to God.

The truth is, every one of us can do better. If we are honest with ourselves, we will know that cooperating with the Holy Spirit will bring blessings to our lives that we could never achieve on our own. Recognizing this is part of the process of maturing spiritually. As Black Christian women, maintaining our health should be a top priority. For this, we must rely on God to empower us so that we can apply His wisdom and understanding. With this in mind, let's look at some ways that we can surrender our decisions over to God and ask Him to help us to change some old habits and replace them with some new routines that will reap great benefits for our health.

THINGS WE CAN CHANGE

Before I address things that we can do something about, let's recognize some things that we simply cannot change. We cannot change the fact that we were born women. And getting older is a natural process that we cannot reverse. If there is a genetic cause for us to gain weight, we can't make that go away either. Women with medical illnesses and those on certain medications may have difficulty losing weight. However, when it comes to being healthy, there are some things we have control over. We can effect change by surrendering our eating habits, along with our sedentary and stressful lifestyles, over to God so that He can work with us to make necessary changes. So let's look at these areas in more detail.

Eating Habits

One of the major sources for weight gain in Black women is poor eating habits and unhealthy food choices. As sisters, we have a tendency to eat too much, too often, and too little of the healthy foods. If we just ate the right foods and only when we were hungry, then the likelihood of us gaining weight would be negligible.

The Bible speaks a lot about food and clearly tells us that eating should not be at the center of our lives. Jesus was very hungry after His forty-day fast in the wilderness. When the Devil tried to tempt Him with food, Jesus said, *"Man does not live on bread alone, but on every word that comes from the mouth of God"* (Matthew 4:4). This means that the center of our lives is Jesus and not food. Even if we are at a stage of hunger, if we let God be the center of our lives, then it is through this relationship with Him that everything else we need will be fulfilled.

When the Israelites left Egypt, they were in the wilderness for forty years and God was in charge of their menu. He fed them with manna and quail and we never heard of them overeating! God never overfed them. In fact, when He provided their first meal, He gave them instructions on how much to eat. Moses spoke to the people and said, *"Each one is to gather as much as he needs"* (Exodus 16:16). Notice that God did not say they should gather as much as they *want.* On the contrary, He told them to gather as much as they *need.* In fact, on that first day when they tried to keep some leftovers for the next day's meal, the food was full of maggots and had a foul odor! Surely, God got His message through and they didn't try that again.

We can learn from the way God fed the children of Israel in the wilderness those years. He fed them with just enough food to satisfy their need. We are to eat only the amount we need to sustain our bodies, which means that we are not to **overeat**. The Word of God offers much wisdom on eating in moderation: *"If you find honey, eat just enough—too much of it, and you will vomit"* (Proverbs 25:16). If we overeat, we are fulfilling our wants and desires and that behavior will cause us to gain weight and increase the risk of developing the diseases we have discussed. Spiritually, we will not be surrendering our lives over to God but making our own decisions for our bodies and that would not be honoring to God.

Moreover, we should **avoid** foods that are high in calories, saturated fats, and sugars. Instead, eating foods low in calories and fats, high in fiber and protein, with at least five servings of fruits and vegetables a day is the wise thing to do.[4]

In the book of Leviticus (11:13–47), God told the Israelites not to eat certain foods; however, in the New Testament, Peter was told by God in a dream that no foods were forbidden. Unfortunately, human nature has a tendency to push beyond safe boundaries—and that's when we get into trouble.

Does this scenario sound familiar to you? A woman may know that she shouldn't be eating cookies, ice cream, cakes, and potato chips. But, if she does eat these things, they should be consumed only in small portions. The problem occurs when she ignores wisdom and consequently develops high cholesterol that leads to hardening of the arteries in the heart, which could subject her to a heart attack. That is the point when she cries out to God for help.

This woman could be any one of us—and we should cry out to God when we are in trouble. But through many reliable sources, such as doctors, nutritionists, and the like, He has already told us not to eat unhealthy foods. Yet, we do it anyway. If we just follow God's direction to eat healthy foods and stay away from the "forbidden foods," the majority of us (including me) would lose weight drastically and lower our cholesterol as well.

Okay, ladies, this is a difficult lesson and it may seem like I've been hard on you. But, know that I include myself in this situation. The reason I can speak to you about it is because I struggle in this area of eating healthy foods. But, it is for our own good that we listen to what God is telling us. Here are some Scriptures to consider about how we should view food and eating properly. As you read them and meditate on them, listen to God as He speaks to you:

SUBJECT	SCRIPTURE
Have a desire for God's Word over food	Job 23:12
Eat for strength and not indulgence	Ecclesiastes 10:17
Don't eat forbidden foods	Isaiah 66:17
Be satisfied with the food Jesus gives you	Matthew 14:15–20
Don't worry about food	Luke 12:22–24
God provides the food on our tables	Acts 14:17

Exercise—Let's Get Physical!

Another way to honor God with our bodies is by keeping them healthy through exercise. There are Scriptures that document people running to give news but the Bible doesn't have much to say about physical exercise except when Paul used an exercise metaphor to describe a spiritual lesson. He does not say that exercise has no benefit, but he tells Timothy: *"For physical training is of some value, but godliness has value for all things, holding promise for both the present life and the life to come"* (1 Timothy 4:8). From this verse, we can surmise that God is not against exercise and acknowledges it has some value. But, it does ***not*** exceed the value of leading a godly life.

We must keep our priorities in order and take Paul's statement on godliness seriously. However, we cannot ignore that there is danger in living a sedentary lifestyle because it does contribute to being overweight and obese. Data collected from the Behavior Risk Factor Surveillance System in 2005 showed that African American women were the least group to report exercise compared to African American men and Caucasian men and women.

The U.S. Department of Health and Human Services recently released a summary of new physical guidelines for exercise starting from age six and up.[5]

These guidelines are based on scientific data that, if followed, can reduce one's risk of developing obesity-related illnesses. One of the highlights was that *some* exercise is better than none! The minimum recommendation for a healthy adult is to exercise two hours and thirty minutes a week with moderate intensity (brisk walking); this has shown to have health benefits. Most of us could achieve this goal simply by walking briskly thirty minutes for five days a week.

You can review all of their recommendations at www.hhs.gov. However, keep in mind that prior to starting any exercise program, anyone who is overweight, obese, or has a medical illness should first seek the advice of their doctor.

Stress: How Do You Spell Relief?

We have already considered the many reasons that contribute to the stresses of life for Black women. The ironic thing about this is that some people can be in a situation and not feel stressed about it while others in a similar situation feel a tremendous amount of stress. It all depends on how you deal with the issues that cause stress in your life. As Christian women, the Word of God is saying to each one of us: *"Cast all your anxiety on him because he cares for you"* (1 Peter 5:7). And we are reminded in Isaiah 26:3 that if we want to be in perfect peace, then we need to keep our minds focused on God.

But, you may ask, how do we do this? Well, experiencing peace from the anxieties of life comes from surrendering our minds to God just as we are encouraged to do with our bodies. We should go to God in prayer daily, read our Bibles, meditate on the Word of God, and fellowship with Him throughout the day. It is through a committed and surrendered relationship with God that He shows us how to deal with the stress. Take it from someone who combats stress in this way. God keeps my stress level down and I'm better able to handle the day-to-day activities when I'm in fellowship with Him throughout the day.

TREATMENT FOR OBESITY

As Black Christian women, relieving ourselves from obesity must be done in an orderly fashion. We must first address the spiritual component of why we are overweight and then we will be able to better address the physical component with the help of God. If we are obese because of our poor eating habits, the first step involves *confession.* As it pertains to food, God tells us not to overeat and to eat the proper foods to keep our bodies healthy.

However, when we find ourselves in violation of God's command, then we must confess our sin, go to God with a humble spirit, and acknowledge our disobedience to His ordinance by not taking care of our bodies as best as we should. Of course, if you have a weight problem through a medical condition, there is no confession to undertake. Just give God thanks, but please read on.

For those of us who know that we have not been as conscientious as we should be when it comes to eating properly, confession is necessary, and God will forgive us. Then we are free to ask God to give us the *desire* to lose weight. But, we have to be sincere and willing to make whatever changes are needed in order to honor Him. God knows our hearts and if we really don't have the desire to change, we will keep on failing until we do (take it from someone who has struggled in this area).

Also, we must have the *right motive* to lose weight. The motive should be to maintain our health so that we honor God with our bodies. The motivation is not to look good or bring glory to ourselves; remember God says, *"Do nothing out of selfish ambition or vain conceit"* (Philippians 2:3). That means we should not desire to lose weight because we will look good and make a good impression on others. Our reason must not be vanity; rather, we should desire to lose weight because God wants us to be healthy and it will prevent certain diseases from harming us.

Once we are armed with the desire and the right motive to lose weight, then we must ask God for the *power* to carry it out. In our own strength we cannot carry out the will of God. Jesus told His disciples, *"apart from me you can do nothing"* (John 15:5). And that applies to us as well. Jesus' statement prompted Paul to say, *"I can do everything through him who gives me strength"* (Philippians 4:13). In essence, the only way we are going to succeed in the effort to overcome obesity (and any other endeavor as Christians) is with the power of Christ resting on us.

Paul learned this when he asked God to remove the thorn in his flesh. God's response to him was: *"My grace is sufficient for you, for my power is made perfect in weakness"* (2 Corinthians 12:9). Paul realized the thorn was making him weak but in his weakness he experienced the power of God resting on him. What a way to experience God's power in our weaknesses! Attempting to eat the proper foods and not overeat can reveal a great source of weakness for most of us. But if we confess this weakness to God and cry out like Paul did, then we should be able to experience the power of God enabling us to carry out His will.

My last suggestion is that you pray and ask God for the **treatment plan** that is specific to your situation. Treatment for you may be as simple as a diet change and an exercise routine or it could involve consultation with a weight management team. There are many organizations out there that are willing to help you lose weight, and the most successful ones are those that help you see weight loss as a permanent lifestyle change. You may be given a plan that involves changes in your diet, starting an exercise program, and participating in behavioral therapy (counseling or support groups).

Some other options at these medical weight loss centers are prescribed medications and surgery to help you lose weight, but these should be done only under the supervision of a doctor. Most of these programs can be found at your local hospitals and some are called wellness or bariatric centers.

If you desire spiritual guidance to help you achieve your goal, I suggest if any psychological counseling is done, it should be through a Christian counselor who will provide Christ-centered counseling. The goal of Christian counseling is to explore the possibilities of why you are overweight and focus your attention on Christ who gives you the power to change and carry out your plan.

Finally, I cannot emphasize enough that anyone who is obese, overweight, or has medical problems should seek the advice of their doctor before changing their diet or starting an exercise program.

CONCLUSION

Yes, it is true that obesity has reached epidemic proportions in America and Black women represent the leading race and gender in obesity and being overweight. Four out of every five Black women are obese or overweight and the statistics are not improving. We as Black women need to stand up and become outraged at these statistics and declare that we will make a change. Our first priority is to honor God and then to improve our health and the health of our families and children.

I have no doubt that through earnestly seeking God in prayer, change will occur. God is able to help us make the change that we so desperately need to get healthy and reduce our risk of developing obesity-related diseases. And for those who may already have diseases in part due to being overweight, don't despair; it is never too late to come to God for help to lose that unwanted weight and improve your present state of health.

For many women, the treatment for obesity and being overweight may be a simple change in food choices and eating habits with an appropriate amount of exercise. For others, it may take an integrated approach at a medical weight-loss center. But, just remember, in order for us to be successful as Christians in weight loss, we must have a true desire to lose weight with the proper motive to honor God and be as healthy as possible. Lastly, we must rely on the power of the Holy Spirit to carry out this new undertaking in our lives. As we do this, the Scripture says we shall find *"grace to help us in the time of need"* (Hebrews 4:16).

REFERENCES

1. U.S. Department of Health and Human Services Office of the Surgeon General http://www.surgeongeneral.gov/topics/obesity. 2001 Report on Overweight and Obesity: "The Surgeon General's Call to Action to Prevent and Decrease Overweight and Obesity." http://www.surgeongeneral.gov/topics/obesity/calltoaction/foreward.htm.

2. American Cancer Society. Atlanta: American Cancer Society; 2007. "Cancer Facts and Figures for African Americans 2007-2008." (Overweight, Obesity and Physical Activity, Figure 9). http://www.cancer.org /downloads/STT/CAFF2007AAacspdf2007.pdf.

3. U.S. Department of Health and Human Services, National Institutes of Health and National Heart, Lung, and Blood Institutes website http://www.nhlbi.nih.gov/educational/hearttruth/about/index.htm.

"The Heart Truth for Women and Heart Disease." "The Heart Truth for African American Women: an Action Plan." NIH publication No: 07-5066 revised December 2007, http://www.nhlbi.nih.gov//educational/hearttruth/downloads/pdf/factsheet-actionplan-aa.pdf.

4. U.S. Department of Health and Human Services website www.hhs.gov. Dietary Guidelines for Americans 2005, http://www.healthierus.gov/dietaryguidelines/released January 12, 2005.

5. U.S. Department of Health and Human Services website www.hhs.gov. 2008 Physical Activity Guidelines for Americans Summary 11/2008 http://www.health.gov/PAGuidelines/.

Chapter Five

RACIAL RECONCILIATION: OUR MINISTRY TO BRIDGE THE GAP

Also, seek the peace and prosperity of the city to which I have carried you into exile. Pray to the Lord for it, because if it prospers, you too will prosper.

JEREMIAH 29:7

Felicia Middlebrooks

When I was asked to write this chapter, my gut wrenched. My first thought was, uh-oh—sackcloth and ashes, sackcloth and ashes! I knew that I couldn't speak to such an emotionally charged issue in my own small strength. Inside, my stomach churned like an overloaded clothes dryer stuffed with long-sleeved shirts—tangled . . . conflicted . . . whites thrown in with rich colors—intertwined in a syncopated rhythm.

I am a Black Christian woman: one who admits to frequent struggles with the issue of racism. Of a truth, I've endured my fair share of sucker punches in corporate America, some public, some private. If perception is reality, then my smoke screens must have been amazingly effective in the workplace; in shopping malls; in neighborhoods where people didn't look like me; in upper-crust restaurants; in boutiques where, from the reception that I received, I clearly didn't belong; even in banks or anywhere else one might simply conduct the daily minutiae of their lives. Nevertheless, I appeared to cope well in the face of racism. Black people tend to do that well. We cope. We survive. We adapt. Yet, through it all—we must be determined to forgive!

However, forgiveness does not mean that we surrender to unbecoming attitudes or aggression but that we wage war within realistic and plausible terms. We must recognize that this struggle is not unlike the spirit of the civil rights movement during the 1960s; namely, we must fight through education and building relationships.

In the course of his civil rights work, Dr. King was jailed fourteen times and stabbed once in the chest. His home was bombed three times. His mail brought a daily, steady stream of death threats and obscenities. Undeterred, he worked twenty hours a day, traveled 325,000 miles, and made 450 speeches throughout the country in the course of one year.

Until his death, he was dedicated to the ideals of persuasion versus coercion and love versus hate. God forbid that I become a scourge to his memory and faith or to all of those who have gone before, willingly laying down their lives so that things could be better for me. God forbid that I or my children succumb to the urge to be bitter or vengeful, lest we too be destroyed by the very spirit that we wage war against! If I teach my children love and tolerance and you do the same, neither of us will have the burden of regret or guilt. Rather, we can anticipate the future with a clear conscience before the Lord.

THE SPIRIT OF RACISM

Racism is a spirit. It is inarguably one of the most clever, dangerous, and divisive tools in Satan's arsenal against contemporary Christianity. It is the antithesis of peace and reconciliation; and if left to fester, it threatens to completely annihilate the brotherhood that God intends for the body of Christ to exemplify and model for the unbelieving world. Destructive at its core, racism is rooted in deception and hatred. It blinds discernment and divides hearts. It sours affection and sears bitterness into the minds of those who would be held captive by its shady principles. Like a parasite looking for a host, racism feeds on ignorance and injustice and flourishes where pride goes unchecked. Furthermore, if it is to be obliterated, then its defeat can only be guaranteed on the spiritual battlefield.

Collectively, the church has taken a backseat in the ongoing struggle for racial reconciliation. Unfortunately, since we ourselves cannot get along, we have given Satan ground and our detractors a reason to question our Christian philosophy and values. With our help, the critics of the contemporary Christian church have had success in writing us off as "hysterical radicals." Although the church at large is guilty because of the backbiting and infighting among us, in particular, Black and White Christians have to assume a great deal of the blame.

Racism is damaging to the body of Christ, primarily because it erodes the very principle of "love thy neighbor as thyself," which Jesus declared to be the second commandment. Further, our society is inundated with a myriad of complex issues that go against the grain of biblical teaching and mandate. These issues can only be effectively challenged when Christians present a united front. However, contemporary Christians have no credibility with many Americans. We are often at odds against each other, and therefore, we can offer no objection regarding abortion, poverty, or same-sex marriage. We have lost our voice because the very thing Jesus said would make the body of Christ distinctive and recognizable to the world, namely—genuine love for one another—is nonexistent.

THE STRUGGLE FOR EQUALITY

For our struggle is not against flesh and blood, but against the rulers, against the authorities, against the powers of this dark world and against the spiritual forces of evil in the heavenly realms (Ephesians 6:12).

African Americans know the pain of racism and partiality all too well. We have held hands and joined hearts, crying out in a collective hope for a brighter future. We have risen up from church pews with our heads bowed in humility, swaying to the rhythms of old Negro spirituals like "O Do Lord, Remember Me!" and hymns such as "I Need Thee Every Hour" or "Pass Me Not, O Gentle Savior." These moving melodies reassure our aching souls that our God would not forget us in our struggles. It's a fight we never asked for but one we seem to find ourselves engulfed in daily. From the time that the slave ships hit America's shores to this present day, we are still fighting. Through this constant struggle, it has become apparent to us that love CON-structs and racism DE-structs. Yet we press on, clinging to what we know.

We are reluctant warriors, scarred by decades-old and present-tense damage to our dignity, our culture, our self-image. All of these detrimental effects are consequences of the pervasive, institutional, and systemic racism that is part and parcel of American society. In fact, racial intolerance is so strong that it even permeates the church. Dr. Martin Luther King Jr. was compelled to make the comment, "The most segregated hour of Christian America is eleven o'clock on Sunday morning." Unfortunately for all involved, that declaration is likely still true today, despite the onslaught of nondenominational megachurches sprouting up around the nation that boast of interracial congregations. Dr. King's words still ring true:

> For many years we have shown amazing patience . . . Our actions must be guided by the deepest principles of our Christian faith. Love must be our regulating ideal.
>
> —DR. MARTIN LUTHER KING

Our struggle for equality has everything to do with having a fervent faith in the Almighty God. We must look to and lean on the God of our weary years to help us overcome the struggles of our faith. For this reason, carrying a Bible, going to church, or quoting Scripture are not the truest tests of our Christianity. These practices don't prove we are Christians any more than sitting in a garage would confirm that you are a car! Rather, our authenticity is validated by our love.

If we are to have a response that mirrors Jesus' example, we must *"speak the truth in love,"* as the apostle Paul described in Ephesians 4:15. And we must do so from a pure heart. We cannot harbor bitterness and allow resentment to go unchecked in our lives. We must confess these and all sins before God. We must be peaceable. Our demeanor must be gentle. We must be approachable, easily entreated, and exhibit a distinct tendency toward kindness. We must love! However, I also have to remind you that our display of love doesn't mean people will automatically resolve their anger toward us. Just know that God will give the power and grace to bear another person's burden of partiality and anger.

We are weary, but still filled with faith that God has not forgotten us. Whether we agree with his politics or not, the historic election of President Barack Obama confirms what our Christian faith teaches us: there really is a *"balm in Gilead"* (Jeremiah 8:22). We should all agree that having an African American man serve as the forty-fourth president of the United States represents a reprieve in terms of racism in our nation, and so we keep moving forward.

If we profess to love God, we will take to heart the exhortation to *"Carry each other's burdens, and in this way you will fulfill the law of Christ"* (Galatians 6:2). Christ knows our pain. And if you're like me and you've felt as though a little bit of you died every time you experienced injustice, then you know Jesus to be a Healer. Behind closed doors, I was fasting and on my knees praying not to hate those who had been partial or shown me hatred. I was asking God for a breakthrough, or at least a glimmer of understanding—anything that would help me rationalize how one group of people could feel like they were somehow more valued by the Creator over other people. All the while, they dare to use the Bible to justify that which is unjust.

Sometimes, I must admit, it's hard to see God through tearstained eyes when racism inflicts its pain. And then I remember Galatians 3:26–28: *"You are all sons of God through faith in Christ Jesus, for all of you who were baptized into Christ have clothed yourselves with Christ. There is neither Jew nor Greek, slave nor free, male nor female, for you are all one in Christ Jesus."* I've had to hold my tongue to circumvent an occasional display of flesh that, unbridled, would likely have resulted in an anger-filled retaliatory diatribe. Instead, I embraced the wisdom of Lawrence J. Peter (1919–1990), educator and management theorist, who once said, "Speak when you're angry, and you'll make the best speech you'll ever regret." That advice would lead me to the nearest empty cubicle or restroom stall to cry out to Jesus. Or, then there were times when I'd simply wait to get home and have an all-out-in-tears-and-gripe session with the Holy Spirit.

God is sovereign. He's perfect and cannot make a mistake. I think about that every time I look at my dark brown skin in the mirror. And I try to remind myself of that truth when I'm challenged by an insensitive remark, a disdainful look, a promotion denied, or an opportunity snatched away. If you wear this skin, then you know exactly what I mean. In America, it carries a heavy price. The consequences of color are real. Good jobs and well-deserved promotions, decent housing, and health care can often be dreams deferred if the dreamer has brown skin.

However, I do believe a fresh wind of change is blowing. I believe a move of the Holy Spirit is ushering in a new day—one filled with hope, love, forgiveness, and reconciliation. I feel a healing coming on and the church must be the conduit of reconciliation. We'll talk more about that a bit later.

The Look and the Pain of Racism

December 4, 2006. It had been a pretty normal news day. We'd had our share of carjackings, murders and attempted murders, awful weather, and bad accidents during the rush hour. After my morning on-the-air ended and midday had crept in with a lull, something happened. Breaking news sent reporters running toward the television monitors in the newsroom. Necks craned. All eyes and ears were fixed on a story coming out of a place called Jena, Louisiana.

Six Black teenagers were charged by police with the beating of a White student at Jena High School. The teens: Robert Bailey, Mychal Bell, Carwin Jones, Bryant Purvis, Jesse Ray Beard, and Theo Shaw had all reached their point of saturation. They told school officials and reporters their beef with the White student, Justin Barker, was not without provocation. These young men had grown frustrated and angry over a number of racially charged incidents that had gone unchallenged at the school. Chief among them—three nooses hung from a tree in the middle of the Jena High School courtyard.

The nooses were a warning to Black children that they were forbidden to take part in the school tradition of sitting beneath a tree like their White peers. The children who carefully and methodically hung the nooses went unpunished. There were no sensitivity training classes or history lessons on the lynching of scores of Black men who were taken secretly in the night—their bodies later being discovered hanging from a tree with that terrible noose around their necks, their genitals having been butchered.

Although this current incident represented an image of horrific proportion, despite the dangerous historical symbolism attached to that rope, it was unjustly dismissed by the Jena school superintendent as a childish prank. The truth is, that noose represented the terror, violence, and threat of death that plagued Blacks in one of the ugliest chapters of American history to ever unfold.

It is every bit as reprehensible as the swastika. The beating victim, Justin Barker, was treated at a local hospital and released. But his attackers were charged with attempted murder and conspiracy. The story made international headlines and evoked bitter debate. As I glanced across the newsroom, there were just a few staffers of color. All of their faces bore a pained expression. Brows furrowed. Eyes narrowed. Heads dropped. They all had *the look*. You know, the look of anguish. The look that says I'm so tired of this fight. The look of hopelessness and despair. The look that struggles to make sense of the senseless. The look that says, not again! It's the same look that was seen on African American faces in the aftermath of the Rodney King trial when four White Los Angeles police officers were acquitted on charges of brutally beating him—a beating witnessed on video around the world.

It's the same look Black faces wore when, on October 23, 1989, the pregnant wife of Boston resident Charles Stuart was shot to death reportedly by a Black man who attempted to rob the couple. The wife and the baby died. The nation was horrified. Stuart, as it was later discovered, wanted out of his marriage, so killed his own spouse and fabricated the entire story. The Black man whom he told police was responsible for his wife's death didn't even exist. Stuart couldn't bear the burden of his own lies and eventually took his own life.

The Don Imus saga evoked that look as well. After their 2007 NCAA Championship loss to Tennessee, the Rutgers University women's basketball team worked to recover from his ugly, insensitive remarks. The CBS network fired Imus, who later apologized. Rutgers basketball coach, C. Vivian Stringer, and her players prayerfully accepted Imus's apology. After meeting with the infamous radio talk show host, Stringer said, "These comments are indicative of greater ills in our culture. It's not just Mr. Imus and we hope that this will be and serve as a catalyst for change. It's time for Americans to hold ourselves to a higher standard."

That look. I have seen it quite often. I've worn it too. More times than I'd like to remember. It's that incredulous expression that prompts you to scramble for your cell phone or smart phone to check your calendar and confirm you're really living in the twenty-first century. So, given many alarming examples, how do we handle these challenges as Christians?

ISSUES OF THE HEART

The bastions of racism and partiality are rooted deeply in the heart. These walls are often more substantial than the Great Wall of China! There are those who call themselves Christians as they stand up to sing and praise God, yet deep down their hearts are filled with hatred and resentment.

Have you ever been to a carnival and visited the game that is played with a life-sized balloon? The object is to knock this huge balloon to the ground. Imagine the frustration of children who hit the balloon continuously until they are out of breath. In their disappointment and inability to win at the game, one might inquire, "Why does it keep coming back up every time I try to knock it down?" Hmm . . . In the most comforting, reassuring voice that can be mustered, Dad explains, "It's not you. It has something to do with what's on the inside of the balloon."

So it is with us. The government can legislate, regulate, and entitle all it wants. But, there is no amount of legislation, regulation, or entitlement that the government can enact to eliminate racism. Racism may fall down, but then it continues to bounce back up. To address the root of the problem, we must go to the core of the issue—our hearts.

WE WRESTLE NOT AGAINST FLESH AND BLOOD

Here's the bottom line: racism is a learned behavior. However, it operates in the spirit realm. So, clearly we're not fighting a battle against flesh and blood (Ephesians 6:12). Be ever mindful that Satan is an opportunist and he works through those who are spiritually weak. This is why it is necessary to be built up in the Spirit of God to stand against evil with the power of a steadfast love.

Our lawmakers, from sea to shining sea, campaign for our votes. They burn the midnight oil to pass complicated bills. They butter us up with promises, most of which they cannot keep. All of these efforts are designed to win our votes so they can keep their jobs. Or perhaps they aspire to loftier political appointments.

However, many of these people are earnest, hardworking, and sincere in their desire to improve the lives of all Americans. To that end, they create laws that help us to enjoy all that this nation has to offer. Laws are also created and passed to help govern the populace, and people face consequences and penalties should they attempt to break them. Sadly, even with such laws in place, you cannot legislate the heart. If mankind had the capacity within themselves to live and love correctly, laws wouldn't be necessary in the first place.

All too often people will attempt to get away with acts tied to negative behaviors, beliefs, and attitudes that are ingrained in their spirits. This becomes a problem when their actions are never corrected or challenged. One of the most common examples of this is seeing a child spew racial hatred. Heads turn and those who bear witness clearly understand the child was exposed to hateful ideology at home. At some point, if that child is not retrained in his or her thinking, then they ultimately grow up to become mean-spirited, hateful, and intolerant adults. Yes, racism is a learned behavior but so is the practice of showing love. Charity begins at home and spreads abroad, as the saying goes.

RACISM AND WORK

During the summer of 2008, CNN successfully pulled off a ground-breaking documentary called "Black in America." One segment of the program focused on Black men and jobs. The report reached a disturbing conclusion. White men with criminal records (a felony conviction) were more than twice as likely to get a callback from a potential employer than a Black man with no criminal record. The stigma tied to the color of their skin was cited as the number one barrier to success. Devah Pater, an associate professor of sociology and faculty associate of the Office of Population Research at Princeton University, says there is very little enforcement in existence for acts of discrimination at the point of hire. He further says the adequate enforcement of antidiscrimination laws represents a vital priority.

Ancella B. Livers and Keith A. Caver, coauthors of *Leading in Black and White: Working Across the Racial Divide in Corporate America,* note that:

> For women the general stereotype is that they are supportive, cooperative, nurturing, less competent than men, and treated as sexual objects. Black women are also forced to deal with a set of perceptions beyond those. They are often considered aggressive and too direct, assertive, and flashy for corporate America. (Livers & Caver 2002)

Unfortunately, the authors said most African American women in the workplace get lumped together in terms of perception. One woman told the authors that there were fifteen other Black professional women in her company, all with different personalities and work styles. But at some point in each of their careers, they were told they were too direct. Sadly, for a woman of color, the stress of trying to survive these predetermined factors and judgment calls can be exhausting and sometimes overwhelming.

BLACK WOMEN CARRY THE BURDEN OF RACISM

In their book *Shifting: The Double Lives of Black Women in America,* co-authors Charisse Jones and Kumea Shorter-Gooden, Ph.D., note that Black women are constantly challenged as they attempt to serve and satisfy others and hide their true selves to placate White colleagues, Black men, and other segments of society. They conclude:

> The ways in which a Black woman shifts have of course changed over time. An enslaved woman or a Black woman living under the heel of Jim Crow would have to shift literally, casting her eyes downward, moving her body off a sidewalk or to the back of a crowded bus when a White passenger came into view. Today, shifting is more subtle and insidious—keeping her silent when a White colleague sexually harasses her, for fear she will not be believed; acting eager but not aggressive at work, so as not to alienate a White boss; and then shifting again at home to appease a Black man who himself has to live with the pain and unfairness of society's prejudices and hate. (Jones & Shorter-Gooden 2003)

Shifting, the authors conclude, is often internal and invisible, and ultimately eats away at a woman's sense of self, often a consequence of living in a world of racial and gender bias. Black women have always been adept. Chameleons. Survivors. We stretch ourselves beyond reason, to prove we're not incompetent. As Christians, we ignore mistreatment so we won't be perceived as threatening or lacking the power or desire to forgive. We churn ourselves into butter to please our bosses, our children, our husbands, and parents—even when we have no more to give. Our health and mental well-being are jeopardized as a result.

The African American Women's Voices Project determined that discrimination was experienced most frequently at work. Sixty-nine percent of respondents told researchers they had experienced racial prejudice at the point of hire, in requests for pay equity, and promotions. For Black Christians, the church is not necessarily a place of refuge. Though most of the women surveyed said they rely heavily on their faith to lift them during difficult times, they felt their gender relegated them to the role of second-class citizens in the traditional Christian church (Jones & Shorter-Gooden 2003). Clearly, we have some issues that require a serious breakthrough.

Black Christian women may have even more difficulty than their secular counterparts. Standard operating procedures might not be appropriate for us. Where we might refuse to engage in a verbal sparring match to resolve a problem at work, sometimes we risk the perception of being viewed as weak, incompetent, or a pushover. If we speak our minds, then we may be perceived as too forward, angry, and aggressive—and certainly not behaving in line with Christ's teachings (Jones & Shorter-Gooden 2003).

SPEAK THE TRUTH IN LOVE

Confrontation is sometimes necessary. Anger is a God-given emotion. What angers you is a key to some injustice you are supposed to correct. If you call yourself a Christian, then that assignment must be carried out in accordance with God's Word, regardless of how your flesh feels about it. No matter how much pride you may take in your level of education or your skill set, intellectual rationale sometimes has very little to do with solving the problem.

How many times has someone reminded us that God is more concerned with our character than our comfort? That means you should be prepared to speak the truth in love as we are advised in Ephesians 4:15, even when it doesn't feel good. Sometimes it means you have to bite your tongue, say nothing, and turn it over to Jesus. Ultimately, this action shows a sign of spiritual maturity.

THE IMPORTANCE OF GODLY CHARACTER

A person's character is the basis for every decision they make. For example, discernment demands that we listen to God's voice. We respond with instant obedience. Our first loyalty is to Christ, not the mandates of contemporary culture or any particular racial or ethnic identity. A person committed to loving her neighbor will take the initiative and show courage and determination. She doesn't wait for White people to extend friendship. Instead she submits herself to the leadership of the Holy Spirit. Our Father has an amazing way of fixing a situation that seems humanly impossible, when we're humble enough to remove ourselves and let God be God. What does God tell us to do when we're mistreated? Of course, He tells us to *"Love your enemies and pray for those who persecute you"* (Matthew 5:44).

Our Faith Is Activated When We Give God What He Requires

Loving our enemies is not optional! In fact, Jesus said, *"'Love the Lord your God with all your heart and with all your soul and with all your mind.' This is the first and greatest commandment. And the second is like it: 'Love your neighbor as yourself.' All the Law and the Prophets hang on these two commandments"* (Matthew 22:37–40).

Love is the difference between practicing true spirituality and mere pseudo-religious behavior. Love is not abstract, but concrete. It isn't difficult to identify. It is obvious, through words and actions. It sets in motion. It is operational. Love is patient and kind. It does not envy. It overlooks fault. Its thoughts are consistent with biblical truth. It puts the needs of others first. Love shows deference. It does not keep a tally of offenses committed against it. Love forgives misdeeds. Love protects and preserves the present, trusts and hopes in the future. Love is preeminent. It is superior to childishness. When love functions in the church, the unit of the whole is superior to individuality.

God Hates Partiality

Actress Daphne Maxwell-Reid can tell us a little something about partiality. You probably remember her pretty face in the CBS TV drama *Frank's Place,* which also costarred her husband, Tim Reid. Or, perhaps she made you laugh in the NBC comedy *The Fresh Prince of Bel-Air.* She also appeared in the movie *Once Upon a Time When We Were Colored.* One day as I picked up the *Chicago Tribune,* which I do every morning, the piece by editorial columnist Dawn Turner Trice immediately got my attention. She was re-counting a very painful experience Mrs. Maxwell-Reid had as a coed attending Northwestern University in 1967. That's when she became Northwestern's first Black homecoming queen. I read the story and wept. Here's the long and short of it:

Daphne Maxwell entered Northwestern University in the turbulent 1960s as a freshman from New York City. She was smart, a National Merit Scholar. No matter. That didn't stop her White roommate from promptly announcing she would NOT be sharing her room with a . . . well, she used the N-word. A little jarred, but undaunted, Daphne toughed it out; she concentrated on her studies and moved on. She ended up with no roommate at all.

A year later, one of her old high school teachers submitted Daphne's picture to *Seventeen Magazine* for its "Real Girl" issue. To Daphne's surprise, she was among three coeds selected. Her Black friends on campus teased her about it and jokingly challenged her to run for Northwestern University Homecoming Queen. She did, and to Daphne's utter surprise, she won!

At the big Homecoming rally, when it was time to enjoy all the pomp and circumstance set aside for the queen and her court, her treatment was anything but royal. The university president wouldn't even look at her. He stood next to her for pictures, holding the crown above her head, and then walked away. There was no applause or fanfare when she and her court were introduced and, to add insult to injury, "Daphne Maxwell" wasn't engraved on the Homecoming cup as tradition would have it. Her name wasn't even included in the Northwestern University 1967–68 yearbook! Never mind that for the previous year an article spanning four pages had been written about her White predecessor. When she inquired about the obvious slight, Daphne was told "It wasn't an important story this year."

All these years later, the pain of that incident never left Daphne. Memories of injustices don't leave our spirits that easily, especially when they're not isolated. The homecoming queen thing was just part of it. Prior to that, there was the rejection she faced from her roommate and the reaction she received when she expressed interest in joining a sorority. There were no Black sororities on campus at the time, so she queried some of the White organizations. Fair-skinned with freckles, Maxwell Reid says she was told by one sorority that they would accept her, as long as she said she was Hawaiian if anyone asked. Lying about who she was, of course, was not an option.

Daphne did graduate from Northwestern with some wonderful achievements, however. She joined other Black students in successfully fighting for the implementation of an African studies program. Daphne also helped to convince school officials that there was a legitimate need for a dorm exclusively for Black females. Most importantly, she completed her studies with a B.A. in interior design and architecture.

Understandably, Daphne Maxwell Reid was the reason her son desired to attend Northwestern a few years ago. However, just as understandably, she forbade it. As a final disappointment in her college experience, the alumna never felt driven to send a contribution to the school after she earned her degree in 1970.

God Does Not Show Partiality

God addressed the issue of partiality because it threatened the very survival of the New Testament church! The entire chapter of Acts, chapter 10 relates the story of Peter and Cornelius. Peter was reluctant to accept Cornelius because he was a Gentile. But God spoke to Peter through a dream about his partiality. In verse 34, Peter responds to the reproof from God in this way: *"I now realize how true it is that God does not show favoritism."*

This passage confirms that God does not endorse partiality, nor is He partial! On the contrary, God invites "whosoever will." In an all-inclusive manner, Jesus described it this way:

* "For whosoever shall do the will of God, the same is my brother, and my sister, and mother" (Mark 3:35 KJV).
* "Whosoever will come after me, let him deny himself, and take up his cross, and follow me" (Mark 8:34*b* KJV).
* "Whosoever therefore shall confess me before men, him will I confess also before my Father which is in heaven" (Matthew 10:32 KJV).

You get the idea. God wants us to adjust our attitudes so that we do not attribute certain characteristics to any particular group of people. He wants us to let go of our preconceived expectations and anticipate that any given person we're looking at is capable of embracing the reality, principles, and truth of Scripture just as we ourselves do.

The apostle Paul responded to the injustice that he perceived in the church:

* "I charge thee before God, and the Lord Jesus Christ, and the elect angels, that thou observe these things without preferring one before another, doing nothing by partiality" (1 Timothy 5:21 KJV).

The words in Greek mean "without prejudice on account of rank, wealth, personal friendship, or predilection of any sort"! Those who profess to be believers must still learn that everyone should be dealt with in the church as she will be dealt with at the judgment seat of Christ.

HOW CAN WE HELP EACH OTHER?

As Black Christian women, our role is to strengthen ourselves and those who will come after us, through prayer, fasting, and a commitment to seeing justice reign. We can accomplish this through our example. In the workplace, we can serve as mentors. I would not have survived my lengthy tenure on the job, with its myriad challenges and difficulties, without the reinforcement of strong men and women in my industry who opened doors for my success. They taught me by example. They prayed for me and kept my sometimes bowed-down head lifted up. I stand on their shoulders. In return, I am always cognizant of my obligation to do likewise for those who come behind me.

In *Across the Divide: Grasping the Black Experience in Corporate America*, authors Ancella B. Livers and Keith A. Caver note:

> Many African Americans feel that their professional responsibility is a mixture of work, personal duty and racial obligation. In fact, more than 90 percent of managers surveyed said they felt obligated to help other African Americans in their organization. This arises from their respect for and feeling of accountability to those who came before them and struggled to get them and other blacks into corporate America. (Livers & Caver 2002)

Black Christian women can also find solace in networking. Networking provides an entrée to opportunities for promotion, interaction with women and men who are like-minded, and the sharing of similar goals. These alliances can be critically important and ensure success of those new to corporate America. When a shared belief in God is at the center of your networking relationships, it's all the more beneficial. Moreover, it's easier to quench Satan's fiery darts in the workplace when you're united with other believers in prayer (Matthew 18:20).

RECONCILIATION: A NONNEGOTIABLE

And he has committed to us the message of reconciliation.
(2 Corinthians 5:19b)

Spenser Perkins, coauthor of *More than Equals: Racial Healing for the Sake of the Gospel,* comments on the disparity between true reconciliation and its opposite, which is found in a form of hypocrisy that rages against God's standard to the highest degree:

> Our witness as Christians labors under the burden of a great historical contradiction: that it is possible to be reconciled to God without loving your neighbor. Whenever Christians have made peace with that fallacy, it has spelled disaster for the world, whether in the form of "born-again" slave holders, hymn-singing Holocaust engineers, apartheid supporters defending their privilege with chapter and verse, or Rwandans loving their culture more than Christ. (Perkins & Rice 2000)

Paul uses the word *reconciliation* first and foremost in regard to the role Jesus Christ had in bringing fallen humanity back to God. The life, death, burial, and resurrection of Jesus guaranteed that we could have a second chance at a relationship with God (Romans 5:10)! Jesus was God's solution to resolve the estrangement between Himself and humanity. The basic meaning of the root word *reconcile* in the Greek is "to change or exchange." Prior to New Testament times, the word was used in classical Greek to describe a change in relationship that brings estranged parties back together.

We are sometimes inclined to meet our enemies "halfway." But, God went ALL the way; He gave 100 percent to exchange our alienation for restoration. We were totally unable to do anything on our own behalf so He took the initiative to bring us back by sending Jesus to bear our penalty. The end result of His work was that we were given an unmerited reprieve. We didn't earn it, can't compensate for it, and we certainly can't maintain it. Our reconciliation was fully God's idea and fully His work.

Reconciliation does not end with our gift of salvation, however, as evidenced by 2 Corinthians 5:18–19: *"All this is from God, who reconciled us to himself through Christ and gave us the ministry of reconciliation: that God was reconciling the world to himself in Christ, not counting men's sins against them. And he has committed to us the message of reconciliation."* Clearly, it is God's intention that the fruit of reconciliation with Him will be reconciliation with all those we are alienated from. Our astonishing salvation has supernatural power to break through any boundary. *"You are all sons of God through faith in Christ*

Jesus, for all of you who were baptized into Christ have clothed yourselves with Christ. There is neither Jew nor Greek, slave nor free, male nor female, for you are all one in Christ Jesus" (Galatians 3:26–28). What the church must understand and come to grips with is that reconciliation is not just some tidy fringe benefit that we have the option to choose or not. Rather, it is a fundamental part of God's plan in regard to humanity.

Reconciliation: Is It Possible?

God gives us impossible visions of future outcomes so that we can only find success in those endeavors through Him! David heard many objections when he demanded to represent Israel against the giant Goliath: "He's too big! You're too small! It can't be done. Others have tried and failed. . . ." Perhaps you have heard the same mammoth doubts and objections in regard to the possibility of destroying the barriers of racism, partiality, and hatred within the church. "This is just the way it is. It's always been this way. We have to just put up with it . . . Do you know how long this problem has existed?"

If David were our contemporary, he would wonder, *how in the world are you all allowing this giant to live in your midst?* Just as he could not conceive of accepting defeat at the hands of Philistia and allowing Goliath to live in his mockery, David would ask us how we can allow the giant of partiality/racism to establish permanent residence in our hearts, homes, churches, and communities.

The wonderful thing about impossibilities that God calls us to is that He does not require anything of us that He is not willing to provide. Since I have acknowledged that God gives us the impossible visions so that we can watch Him bring them to fulfillment, let's appeal to God with some specific requests regarding our charge to be reconcilers.

Please Pray . . .

That the church will:
* triumph over principalities and powers of division and strife
* experience harmony
* foster peace among us and deny our ambitious desires as Scripture dictates: "be at peace with each other" (Mark 9:50*b*)

When Our Prayers Are Answered . . .

Christians individually will exchange the following tendencies of our old nature to embrace who we are in Christ:

- laziness for initiative
- arrogance for humility
- belligerence for love
- indifference for resolve
- filthy communication for courteous speech
- anger, wrath, and malice for forgiveness
- blasphemy for a wholesome fear of God

Just as God rewarded Nehemiah's prayer to rebuild the walls of Jerusalem, He will honor our resolve to plunder the walls in the church today that separate us and hinder our effectiveness. Like Nehemiah, we must stand in the gap through effectual, fervent, persistent prayer.

A DIFFERENT MIND-SET

David refused to entertain the negative comments he received; he had a different mind-set. The reconciler has a different mind-set; she is a woman of faith and has a different "flavor." The reconciler is a person of godly character. When met with all the exceptions and objections, the reconciler relies on her courage and sense of purpose to accomplish her goals. She is uncompromising. The mind-set of Christians committed to reconciliation is to find common ground. Our identity in Christ should evoke a spirit of unity and dispel all objections to it. David purposed in his heart to do what was required to defeat the giant in his life. Likewise, we must share David's resolve in regard to the giant of racism. Racism is not too big of a giant to fight; in fact, it's too big to miss!

Reconciliation: Our Duty

Performing our duty communicates to society that our Christianity reflects God's characteristic of integrity. When what we think, say, and do are all the same, we are people of integrity. Our duty as Christians is defined in

Romans 12:1 (KJV) as fulfilling our *"reasonable service."* This is what we owe God. Duty is a transition of our allegiance from being self-centered to Christ-centered. If knowledge teaches man his rights, rights teach man his duty. If a right exists, then there is a duty, or responsibility, that coexists.

In regard to reconciliation, we have a right to be friends with whoever we will. But, we have a duty to love all the brethren. Love, in the context of Christianity, is our duty. We must persevere in upholding our responsibility to Him who gave it to us. Duty is ours. Results belong to God.

The Rest of Daphne Maxwell-Reid's Story

The saga of Daphne Maxwell-Reid as a coed in 1967 at Northwestern recently came to the attention of members of the Northwestern University Black Alumni Association. The association informed the school's current president, Henry Bienen, who decided to try and make things right.

Daphne was invited to attend homecoming, to witness firsthand the social, cultural, and academic progress that has been made since 1970. What a nice gesture. Although it is nearly thirty years late, it's nonetheless significant. Daphne graciously accepted the invite. Hopefully, her return to the campus allowed her the long overdue opportunity to be reconciled with her alma mater.

Progress in the Works . . .

In what was a hotly contested presidential race, America made history by electing the first African American president of the United States. Barack Obama was educated in the most prestigious schools in the nation. He is a father, husband, and a Christian. In the end, his ethnicity was of no consequence. The hot-button issue of economics that affects all recession-weary Americans became the chief factor in the voters' mood at the polls.

People were hungry for something new and different. They were going broke. During the week of October 20, 2008, *Time* magazine reported accurately on the cover of its campaign special issue: "The Economy Is Trumping Race." If your house is burning, does it really matter what race the firefighters are?

Now, more than ever I think we are seeing signs of a great change sweeping across America. It gives me hope, a hope that I don't think I've ever experienced before. I believe the changes that need to take place in the hearts and minds of our nation will be ushered in by young people unscathed by the remnants of ignorance, evil, and injustice that permeate our society. It will be the youth who will quickly dismiss any notion of mistreatment of one individual or group because their physicality doesn't fit what is deemed acceptable.

There is also a remnant among my generation who is just simply ready for change, as evidenced by the landmark election of our forty-fourth president. God never intended for the body of Christ to live in a collective rage over color. He intends for us to embrace our differences that, by the way, exist by His divine design. He would have us love each other—with no preconditions. It's high time for those who say they belong to Christ to honor that commandment of love. As for those of us who have been victimized and have suffered the ravages of racism, we must be willing to crucify our flesh daily, forgive those who hurt us, enlighten our offenders as they allow us an opportunity to engage in healthy dialogue, and keep our focus fixed on the One who sees all things.

God fully expects us to trust Him as we attempt to walk in integrity. He's already empowered us to do just that (2 Peter 1:3).

REFERENCES

Jones, C., and K. Shorter-Gooden. 2003. *Shifting: The Double Lives of Black Women in America.* Based on the African American Women's Voices Project. New York: HarperCollins.

Livers, A., and K Caver. 2002. *Leading in Black and White: Working Across the Racial Divide in Corporate America.* San Francisco: Jossey-Bass.

Livers, A., and K. Caver. 2002. *Across the Divide: Grasping the Black Experience in Corporate America.* San Francisco: Jossey-Bass.

Perkins, S., and C. Rice. 2000. *More than Equals: Racial Healing for the Sake of the Gospel.* Downers Grove, Illinois: Intervarsity Press.

Time magazine. "Why the Economy Is Trumping Race." Special issue cover: October 20, 2008. http://www.time.com/time/covers/0,16641,200810 20,00.html.

Chapter Six

MONEY AND FINANCIAL
FITNESS: STRETCH,
SAVE, AND SHARE

When times are good, be happy;
but when times are bad, consider:

God has made the one
as well as the other.

ECCLESIASTES 7:14

Lisa A. Crayton

Nontraditional family dynamics have long positioned Black women as heads of our household; and, by default, those of us who assume that position carry out the role of primary money manager. Even if we share the responsibility of household management with a mate, we must be adept at stretching limited funds to meet seemingly exhaustive needs. However, most women struggle with this task because we haven't really acquired the needed skills to wisely manage our family finances. When our financial house is not in order, we live and die in debt, leaving behind little or no financial inheritance for our children. Our loved ones are then left to cope with a legacy rife with irate creditors, steep burial fees, and bleak futures.

Perhaps you witnessed your parents living in similar financial straits and vowed to live differently. Either secretly, or openly, you promised to manage your family finances more strategically, and thus assure a better, brighter financial future and legacy for yourself and your children. Well, I believe that I can safely say that we all share in the desire to achieve that goal. But, some of us fulfilled our vow, while others have not. Waging war on poor financial decisions and developing a lifestyle of good money management has been for most Black women, continually, a losing battle. Whatever the case, recent economic events have most of us lamenting. And we find ourselves echoing Job's sentiment: *"What I feared has come upon me; what I dreaded has happened to me. I have no peace, no quietness; I have no rest, but only turmoil"* (Job 3:25–26).

ECONOMIC STIMULUS?

"It was the best of times, it was the worst of times." The opening line from *A Tale of Two Cities* by Charles Dickens aptly sums up the American economy in 2008. Politically, it was the best of times. America made the historic decision to elect its first Black president. The *world* rejoiced when that possibility became reality with the election of President Barack Obama.

Financially, it was the worst of times, with America experiencing catastrophic events in the investment, banking, and real estate sectors of business. As events unfolded, it quickly became evident that America's economy would likely not recover until 2010—or beyond. In the midst of the economic turmoil, one truth prevailed: money matters.

Whether rich or poor, Americans, in general, must reexamine the way we handle money. We have been forced to question more closely the way in which key officials approach local and national monetary policies. On the other hand, some good has come out of the present economic climate as it offers an ideal opportunity for us to become financially fit.

A Vicious Cycle

Ironically, while most of us are too young to remember the Great Depression as anything more than a history lesson in grade school, some of us do remember the financial crises in the 1980s. I certainly do.

Last year when many renowned financial services firms closed and numerous banks faced insolvency, I felt as if I were experiencing a bad case of déjà vu circa 1988. When my historic Wall Street bank employer toppled in a hostile takeover, everyone was saying that it couldn't happen. But it did. Within weeks of the deal, I narrowly avoided a pink slip by quickly landing a position with a prestigious financial services firm. However, I was promptly laid off when that firm filed bankruptcy. Following a deluge of risky real estate investments, it had rapidly lost money in an imploding real estate market.

Fast-forward to 2009. In addition to other hard-hit industries, the legal field has experienced its fair share of mergers and insolvencies. Once again we are in the midst of yet another industry hard-hit by a downturn in financial markets. As I witnessed these events firsthand, I could not help but marvel about the cyclical nature of money matters. Yet, these cycles are consistent and predictable within the capitalist monetary system.

Indeed, when it comes to money matters, the more things seem to change, the more they stay the same. For example, in many respects the events leading up to last year's emergency economic recovery package mirrored those our nation faced at the onset of the Great Depression in 1929. How had we come so far only to once again face such devastating financial dilemmas? The answer lies in risky investments, hefty executive bonuses, as well as personal and national debt, among other things. More so, the culprit is an American dream that increasingly places too much emphasis on material acquisition. Resulting money-related concerns turn that dream into a nightmare for many Americans. What a vicious cycle!

BLACK WOMEN AND MONEY

Is money a major concern of Black women? Definitely. In fact, a 2008 study by financial services giant ING found that Black women fretted more about money than they did about their health, job, appearance, or relationships. The survey, conducted in partnership with *Essence* magazine, surveyed more than 1,400 women: 1,000 preretirement Black women and 454 non-Black women. Its findings highlighted a number of familiar money matters:

Family obligations. Some 47 percent of Black women said family obligations blocked their ability to achieve a "desired lifestyle."

Loans to others. More than 50 percent of women loaned $500 or more to family and friends in the previous year, while more than a third said they had loaned over $1,000 to family or friends in that same period. Note what Scripture has to say about borrowing and lending money: *"The rich rule over the poor, and the borrower is servant to the lender"* (Proverbs 22:7). While the survey did not indicate whether any of those loans were paid back, my experience is that oftentimes such advances are not.

To eliminate frustration on my part and guilt on a family member or friend's part, I carefully consider whether God is directing me to help someone financially. If He is, I consider such loans a gift to the lender, and I don't worry about whether I will receive it back. This approach may not work for everybody, but it can improve one's ability to "sow" into the lives of family and friends as an extension of God's love and mercy to them. It also brings balance to the borrower/lender relationship.

Spending habits. Some 68 percent of respondents said the state of the economy does not affect their spending. Whether the economy is good or bad, they buy what they want. Meanwhile, about 40 percent said they shop "to cheer themselves up." At the same time, 41 percent said they feel guilty about spending on expensive brands.

Savings. While 25 percent of women said they do not save any money each month, more than 50 percent said they live "paycheck to paycheck."

Some positive results from the ING/*Essence* survey include:

Investing. Two-thirds of Black women said they own a retirement account 401(k), 403(b), or IRA; while 28 percent said they own individual bonds and stocks and 23 percent own mutual funds. (Admittedly, in each category, the percentage of Black women investing was lower than that of other women, but those Black women who do save can be applauded for their investment efforts.)

Giving. More than 70 percent of Black women said they believed giving money to their place of worship is important. That number is significantly higher than the 42 percent of all other women who said the same.

BALANCING ACTS

According to authors Ted Klontz, Rich Kahler, and Brad Klontz, money can be used as a "tool to help us achieve authenticity and our most important life aspirations." They go on to say, "Like any tool, it's important to learn how to use it wisely" (Klontz, Kahler & Klontz 2006). Wise use of our resources hinges on balance. For starters, we need to balance our *view* of money. While it was initially designed to be a basic tool for exchanging goods and services, money has morphed into something much more complex. For some, money is a *lifeline* that connects them to fame and fortune. For others, it is a *handcuff* that secures their control over other people's affection and lives. Many others use it as a *narcotic* that influences and alters mood, thinking, and behavior (Klontz, Kahler & Klontz 2006).

Moreover, we need to bring balance to our understanding of *why* we mishandle money matters. At the least, we must comprehend the potential reasons why we could mismanage money. Bert Whitehead, the author of *Why Smart People Do Stupid Things with Money*, calls these blunders "financial dysfunctions" (Whitehead 2007). They are "financial choices and strategies that people believe are effective but that actually impede their financial progress" (Whitehead 2007). Whitehead cites four springboards to those dysfunctions:

1. Lack of awareness of your financial personality
2. Relying on factors outside of your control
3. Inability to benchmark progress
4. Using tools and strategies designed for other people's needs (Whitehead 2007)

Here is another thought to consider: As difficult as the truth may be to swallow, and whether we are a victim or seemingly victor, the *love of money* could be the underlying root of one's dissatisfaction. Scripture teaches us, *"For the love of money is a root of all kinds of evil. Some people, eager for money, have wandered from the faith and pierced themselves with many griefs"* (1 Timothy 6:10). Topping the list of those "griefs" that God's Word refers to are broken relationships, financial troubles, food disorders (including obesity), stress, and stress-related illnesses.

Moreover, we are all probably aware of a syndrome that is commonly referred to as "shop till you drop." If we want to counteract an overzealous affection for money indulgences such as this, then sidestepping that kind of money-related grief and its often regrettable aftereffects requires wise spending. Three areas come into play in regard to our spending decisions: attitude, consistent budgeting, and overall commitment to spending money wisely.

Attitude. The adage "attitude determines altitude" aptly applies to how we perceive money. "Generally speaking, all money beliefs are a variation on one of two themes: Money is evil; money is good. Whether we worship money or hate it, when we hold it responsible for our happiness we give it power. Whether consciously or subconsciously, we choose the role money plays in our lives. So, we—not our money or lack of it—are solely responsible for our attitudes, beliefs, actions, and happiness" (Hunt 2008).

Essentially, if we consider money simply a medium of exchange, we will prudently use it to:

1. attain the things we need for daily living
2. save for future needs or desires
3. help others

On the other hand, if our attitude is skewed, our actions will mirror our "stinking thinking" and result in:

1. Compulsive spending
2. Limited or nonexistent savings
3. An inability to help others (or possibly helping others at our own detriment, as the ING survey revealed)

Furthermore, much of the misuse of money stems from childhood issues related to the way our families handled money. Authors Klontz, Kahler, and Klontz (2006) call these messages from our developmental years "money scripts," and they note:

Very early in life, people begin to internalize messages about money's purpose—how it works, what it promises—its overall significance—and develop their relationship to it. Since children can't fully grasp adult reality, they translate what they see and hear into unconscious rules about life, including any internalized messages about money. These messages about money, or money scripts, don't necessarily reflect reality from an adult perspective. Instead, they may represent only a distorted or partial truth as seen through the eyes of a child. As children grow into adulthood, they often behave as though these partial truths are absolute truths. They may find themselves unable to change destructive behaviors that, at a very basic level, somehow feel right and make perfect sense. . . . Our deepest, most ingrained money scripts are often formed by . . . financial trauma. (2006)

Rediscovering those initial traumas and readjusting our attitudes facilitates effective money management. Black Christian women can find biblical help for doing so by studying relevant, money-related Scriptures. There is no lack of instruction, since money is much talked about in the Bible! Use a print or online concordance and search such terms as "money," "wealth," "steward," or "riches." Consider committing the results of some of these word meanings to memory. Perhaps you might even use your favorite Bible verse on the good stewardship of money as a screen saver on your computer.

Also study Jesus' money-related parables: the unmerciful servant (Matthew 18:23–35); vineyard workers (Matthew 20:1–16); talents (Matthew 25:14–30); moneylender (Mark 13:34–37); rich fool (Luke 12:16–21); prodigal son (Luke 15:11–32); and wise manager (Luke 16:1–8).

Finally, the financial dealings of biblical characters offer money lessons from which we can acquire wisdom or learn to avoid their folly and mishaps. Those characters include Joseph (Genesis 37; 39–45; 47); King Solomon (1 Kings 3:1–15; 10:23–29; 11:4–8); the widow of Zarephath (1 Kings 17); Ananias and Sapphira (Acts 5:1–11); Dorcas (Acts 9:36–42); and the Macedonian church (2 Corinthians 8:1–5).

Budgeting. Balancing budgets remains a basic tenet of effective money management. It encompasses our view of priorities and how we regularly allocate income to them.

It is true that competing needs vie for our limited incomes. Therefore, getting the most for our money requires a realistic, prayerful approach to balancing—or prioritizing—needs versus wants. This is such an elementary money management strategy, but many of us fail to apply it to our lives. Be aware, when it is left unchecked, unbalanced spending, which is evidenced by compulsive spending and overreliance on credit cards, often short-circuit our best intentions.

I discovered this as a new college graduate. Back then, I racked up loads of debt buying expensive clothing that I did not need but sorely wanted. Case in point: my desire for top-of-the-line pantyhose, undergarments, and lingerie. They set me back hundreds of dollars a year, but lasted no longer than their cheaper counterparts (regardless of the price tag, pantyhose rip!). Today, I opt for less expensive alternatives or shop for pricier ones only during sales. Many times I take advantage of using a print or online coupon for even more savings.

Our grandmothers would have called this approach being "frugal," but many in our generation shun the term, equating it with a less than enviable lifestyle. Yet, there are great benefits to being frugal. Author Mary Hunt wisely says, "Frugal doesn't mean tacky, frumpy or stingy. It means we don't spend money we do not have yet" (Hunt 2008).

Our emotions can prove to be huge budget-busters. Women tend to use money as an antidote to rejection or relationship angst. As Mary Hunt (2008) also points out, "There's a real danger in using money to alter our moods because it is very easy to become addicted to the act. We are easily addicted beings. Some people medicate strong feelings with a drug of choice, others with a compulsive behavior. For many women, shopping is an effective way to deal with fears and feelings of insignificance and loneliness. They buy something pretty in the same way a mother hands a pacifier over to a fussy baby."

God never intended us to use money as a pseudo *"balm in Gilead"* (Jeremiah 8:22). Ever-ready to heal our emotional traumas, He lovingly reveals our self-defeating behaviors and offers lasting solace. So, rather than shopping until you drop, do this:

> *Trust in the Lord with all your heart and lean not on your own understanding; in all your ways acknowledge him, and he will make your paths straight. Do not be wise in your own eyes; fear the Lord and shun evil. This will bring health to your body and nourishment to your bones.* (Proverbs 3:5–7)

Commitment. Jump-start your commitment to sound money management principles, including those mentioned above. There are two simple steps: First, make a list of the short- and long-term financial objectives you'd like to achieve in the next one, five, and ten years. Writing down your goals compels you to think about how you want to spend your money—and when. For example, if you want to save for a child's college education, then you know you'll need to allocate significant sums of money over a specific time period to achieve that purpose.

Second, assign realistic goals to each objective. Keep in mind that a realistic goal is one that is easily reachable, based on your time, talents, and resources that are available *today*.

Glinda Bridgforth (2000) explains the importance of setting goals. "A critical part of a successful financial program is having a goal or objective that motivates and energizes you. It's not enough to just say 'I want to be debt free' or 'I want to save money.' Having a compelling reason [*why*] you want to become debt free or setting a [motivating] goal for which you are saving money creates a burning desire that gives you the motivation to move forward when you get tired and frustrated or when you feel you're not progressing fast enough."

Above all, let the Word of God be your guiding force and rely on God's counsel: "*Commit to the Lord whatever you do, and your plans will succeed*" (Proverbs 16:3). As you do, keep in mind that life is all about seasons (Ecclesiastes 3:1). It is a great reminder to think before we shop, and pray before we buy. When you are faced with a decision whether to spend or not, ask yourself one of the following:

- Is it really time to buy this?
- Why am I really charging this item today?
- Can this purchase wait until tomorrow, next week, or next month?
- How will this shipwreck my money for this month?
- Will God be pleased with me using my money this way?

FINANCIAL CONFIDENCE

Interestingly, the ING survey proved that while Black women perceive ourselves as financially confident, we don't always handle our money responsibly. Yet, *responsible* behavior is a keystone to financial *confidence*. As Mary Hunt (2008) describes, "A financially confident woman is a woman who has the knowledge, ability, and desire to behave in a financially responsible manner." To achieve financial confidence, Hunt suggests that women:

1. Investigate how financially confident women behave.
2. Eliminate habits based on false money beliefs.

3. Imitate and practice those positive and beneficial behaviors so
    frequently that they become almost automatic.

Because understanding of the first of these suggestions paves the way for
the next two, we'll focus on how financially confident women behave. Essentially, women who are financially confident focus on three pillars of effective
money management. These women: 1) spend wisely, 2) save a portion of all
monies received, and 3) share with others. As we strive for financial confidence by following these steps, which are further discussed below, let's do our
part and trust God to do His. If we do this, we will have the ability to acknowledge like the apostle Paul that *"our competence comes from God"*
(2 Corinthians 3:5).

A Plan to Spend

As previously mentioned, budgeting is a key to spending wisely. Regarding budgets, Bridgforth (2000) chides:

> Often African American women are put off by budgets because we don't
> want any ceilings put on our spending. . . . The term budget has a nega-
> tive connotation and feels limiting, restricting, and more or less cast in
> stone with no flexibility because we commit to it on paper. We work too
> hard to feel lack, deprivation, or extreme sacrifice. We also fear making a
> budget because it might show that we don't have enough money to meet
> all our wants and needs. Or because we're afraid to face our out-of-
> control spending patterns. Since most of us have on some occasion tried
> to follow a budget, it also feels like a setup for failure.

Viewing a budget as a "spending plan" versus a money diet helps Black
women get a grasp on budgeting. "A spending plan [versus a money diet], on
the other hand, feels more positive. By definition, a plan is always proactive
and empowering. . . . The purpose of the spending plan is not to limit our
spending but to identify what we need for a quality of life that has a sense of
balance and well-being. It's a blueprint to help keep our financial house in
order" (Bridgforth 2000).

Keys to an effective spending plan include: 1) recognition of *limited* monthly income from all sources (full- and part-time salary, child support, alimony, small business ventures, and so on); 2) inclusion of *ongoing* monthly expenses (mortgage or rent, car payment, child care, child's tuition, and so on); 3) dedication to planned giving (tithes and charitable contributions); and, 4) anticipation of planned savings (including those made by payroll deduction). Monies allocated for giving, saving, and expenses must be deducted from net income before a true picture of any "disposable" income emerges. Including a "fun money" category provides ready cash for personal or family outings. However, be careful not to sock more money away for entertainment purposes than you do for meeting your daily needs.

A "rainy day" fund also remains a vital part of any spending plan. Used for emergency purposes, this money provides a safety net for unplanned expenses, such as repairs to vehicles or homes, or expenses related to unexpected illnesses. Such monies reduce or eliminate the stress, aggravation, and fears that arise when money is not available to handle such emergencies.

A balanced checking account evidences a well-executed spending plan. Whether you balance yours in a traditional checkbook register or on a computer spreadsheet is not as important as keeping the balance updated regularly. Opting for online banking provides a fast, efficient method of doing so.

Even if you prefer receiving a printed statement, consider using online banking to balance your checkbook. Check transactions weekly or biweekly to reconcile your checkbook, especially for ATM transactions (including withdrawals and debit purchases) you may have overlooked. If paying bills is a challenge, also opt for online bill payment.

Make a Commitment to Debt Reduction

Finally, debt tops the list of impediments to wise spending. Whether debt becomes a blessing or curse depends on how we use it and its overall impact on our quality of life. Hence, we hear the terms "good debt" and "bad debt." Payday loans and high-interest credit cards fall within the bad debt category. Car loans and mortgages, conversely, have long been considered "good" debt. The subprime mortgage debacle has demonstrated how easily debt can shift from beneficial to harmful. Many home owners holding these mortgages lost their homes to foreclosures once interest rates skyrocketed. By all accounts, however, subprime mortgages represent a risky rather than wise credit option;

underscoring the truth of the old adage: "If it sounds too good to be true, it probably is."

A Penny Saved . . .

During the height of last year's financial meltdown, investors who had stored monies in investment accounts, including 401(k) and other retirement plans, saw their balances plummet overnight. In many cases, even average investors lost thousands of dollars. As financial markets floundered, experts advised investors, "Don't stop saving!" That seemingly paradoxical advice reinforced the importance of saving money, regardless of current economic conditions.

As the ING survey indicated, various factors hinder savings goals. Few of us can attest to having saved at least three months' salary, which is a basic emergency fund balance needed to offset employment loss or a health crisis. But even in the face of recession, however, there are steps we can take to meet savings goals. We might:

Use payroll deduction. The old adage "out of sight, out of mind" may make saving money easier. For every pay period, consider setting aside a certain percentage or a specific dollar amount from your gross or net salary. Have these monies deposited in a savings account (albeit, most don't yield high interest as in the past, but they are still useful) or another checking account separate from the one you use regularly.

Collect loose change. Many of us regularly drop loose change and one-dollar bills in jars, piggy banks, and other containers around the house or on the job. Sometimes these savings are lost to theft or we use them on unplanned purchases. It would be better to deposit the funds in a banking account where they will be safe for long-term savings or specific short-term goals. (Roll the coins yourself or use the automated counting machines that are placed in supermarkets.) Several years ago, I earmarked my son's large piggy bank as his "fun money" for our vacation to Orlando. For months, we dropped coins and bills in the bank. A week before the trip, we rolled the coins, gathered all the money, and took it to the bank. To my son's surprise, we returned with slightly less than $75—a virtual windfall for an eight-year-old!

Beef-up retirement accounts. Most working people are looking forward to retiring some day. And retirement is within reach for many of us. How comfortably we spend those "golden years" will depend on how much we invest today for tomorrow. For that purpose, you may want to consider setting aside more rather than less money in a retirement account. On the other hand, if you have yet to set up a 401(k) account at work, do so. Many employers still contribute profit-sharing monies into accounts for employees participating in such plans.

Analyze investments. Only you know how much risk you can handle when investing. But, last year's financial crises proved that oftentimes less risk is better when it comes to preventing large investment-related losses. Thus, consider analyzing the investment mix of your 401(k) and other investments to determine if perhaps previous allocations no longer meet your long-term investing needs. Depending on the level of your comfort with your own financial intelligence, you may want to get some expertise from a financial consultant, someone who can help you make the appropriate decisions based on your personal needs.

Save or invest extra funds. While using extra income to pay off credit cards and other debt is a lofty idea, too many of us max out on debt soon afterward. Test yourself on this idea. When you don't have disposable cash readily on hand, the temptation to "charge" certain items that you could really do without might land you back into debt again. Instead, it would be better to set aside all or a portion of your financial bonuses, tax refunds, and other monies as savings for your future.

Get help. Remember to solicit the help of investment planners, CPAs, and other financial experts to help you analyze your present bottom line. There are many reliable resources to tap into as you strategize ways to better save for the future.

A HEART TO GIVE

The ING survey identified African American women as having a significant propensity to give. Many of us know well the delight of giving to family and friends as well as strangers. However, some of us struggle with giving; we are concerned that it will limit what we can spend on ourselves. Regardless of where you fall on the giving continuum, consider Jesus' words in Luke 6:38: *"Give, and it will be given to you. A good measure, pressed down, shaken together and running over, will be poured into your lap. For with the measure you use, it will be measured to you."*

While not being limited to financial gifts, this verse mirrors Acts 20:35, *"It is more blessed to give than to receive."* It is a giving principle that the apostle Paul attributes to Jesus.

Here is some great advice, "If you've never been one to habitually give, get ready to experience a whole new dimension in your life. . . . If you want your life to have purpose, your finances to come into balance, and your faith to increase, become a giver" (Mary Hunt 2008). Indeed, she says, "I would strongly suggest you add this to your personal belief system: 'Part of everything I have is mine to give away. Giving is an expression of my gratitude, a drain for my greed, and the way I keep my life in balance'" (Hunt 2008).

Last year, many nonprofit organizations saw drastic reductions in donations as the economy slid deeper into recession. While it is a natural tendency to withhold financial (and other) gifts at times like these, know that those gifts are the mainstay of nonprofit organizations, including our churches. Thus, now more than ever before, consider ways you can give—despite the economy.

One biblical solution is to follow Isaac's example. In the midst of famine, *"Isaac sowed in that land"* (Genesis 26:12 KJV). In order to sow seed in a land ravished by famine, Isaac had to sow by faith, not by sight, thus overlooking the parched ground. Further, he had to potentially ignore the stares and comments of others around him who had to consider him crazy for even *thinking* about sowing seed during such a time.

Likewise, we must do the same as we faithfully give tithes and offerings to our local churches, as well as other ministries and charitable organizations. How? We must reinforce our heart to give by doing the following:

1. *Renew Our Minds.* It is so easy to adopt a "famine mind-set," bemoaning the economy and any negative fallout. Such behavior does not exhibit faith, change the economy, or draw people closer to God. Rather, let's weather the present economic conditions like good soldiers of Christ. Let's renew our minds, embracing Philippians 4:8 (KJV): *"Whatsoever things are true, whatso-*

ever things are honest, whatsoever things are just, whatsoever things are pure, whatsoever things are lovely, whatsoever things are of good report; if there be any virtue,
and if there be any praise, [let us] think on these things."

2. *Discern the Season.* Many a financial plan is wrecked by pursuing "off-
season" actions. Perhaps it's not the time to buy a new car, new home, or take
that pricey vacation. Perhaps it's not the time to rack up additional debt by re-
financing your home (even if you could find a lender!). Perhaps it *is* the time
to put the credit cards on ice and only use cold cash (or "hard" plastic, debit
cards). Perhaps it *is* the time to sow and not hold on to your "one day I'll wear
this" clothing items that you haven't worn since you purchased them years
ago. Perhaps it *is* the time to sow rather than keep the tithe. We must understand that, as Christians, we are especially privileged to further the gospel in
this fashion: *"From everyone who has been given much, much will be demanded;
and from the one who has been entrusted with much, much more will be asked"*
(Luke 12:48).

3. *Focus on the Important, Not the Urgent.* Now more than ever, it's important to discern God's leading, and follow it. According to Charles Hummel, author of *Tyranny of the Urgent,* "We live in constant tension between
the urgent and the important. The problem is that many important tasks need
not be done today or even this week. [In our minds, we think that] extra hours
of prayer and Bible study, a visit to an elderly friend, or reading an important
book are all activities that can usually wait a while longer. But often urgent,
though less important, tasks call for immediate response . . . endless demands
pressure every waking hour" (Hummel 1994).

4. *Seize the Moment.* Opportunities don't cease to come our way simply because the economy is lagging. In fact, sometimes the effects of a sluggish economy can do just the opposite and spur opportunities. For example, rising food
prices provide ample incentive to cook more nourishing meals in order to cut
back on fast-food dining. Job cuts provide an opportunity for discharged employees to embrace their goals and dreams. It gives them the opportunity to
consider following those dreams rather than chasing after the "almighty dollar." At the same time, employees who were retained are allowed to stretch
and grow professionally.

5. *Recognize Famine Does Not Mean Forsaken.* The truth is, nothing—and
that includes economic downturns and related money worries—can separate

us from God's love. Furthermore, nothing surprises God. While He may not always intervene in our affairs when we want Him to, God is omniscient and omnipotent. He knows our heartaches and dreams. He sees our tears, hears our cries, and promises never to leave or forsake us—not even during recession.

6. *Expect the Unexpected.* It is comforting to read Scripture and observe God's unusual, yet timely help in troubled times. In many instances, His help is so much more awesome than what we had hoped. Scripture does not tell us what Isaac's expectations were when he sowed. It is a good chance that in a time of famine, he was not *really* expecting a full harvest, since a partial harvest would have ensured enough food for his family, servants, and livestock. Whatever his expectations, *"Isaac planted crops in that land and the same year reaped a hundredfold, because the Lord blessed him. The man became rich, and his wealth continued to grow until he became very wealthy. He had so many flocks and herds and servants that the Philistines envied him"* (Genesis 26:12–14). Our giving may not make us rich, but it will continue to help others experience the hand of God during tough times.

OUR SAFE HARBOR

When Isaac viewed his future in a land of famine, he chose to run away. God thwarted that plan, promising to bless him if he stayed put. Similarly, our knee-jerk, runaway reactions to recession may include a rush to file for bankruptcy, pull equity out of mortgages for one reason or another, or remove monies from retirement plans to finance seemingly important short-term goals. On the giving front, we might be tempted to envision our future as one where we withhold financial contributions to assure our own pressing needs are met.

Generally, those reactions clearly pinpoint a shortsighted present-day focus, rather than a promising future focus. Yet, the key to effective money management has always been to focus on the future and not the present. Therefore, to achieve success, the wise way is to set our sights on long-term goals instead of temporary pleasures.

This key of wisdom unlocks doors to two other important financial principles: liquidity and safety. A "liquid" investment is one that provides quick and easy access to cash. A safe investment is one that minimizes risk while preserving principal, initial monies invested. "Safe harbor" investments are designed to provide a 100 percent guarantee that investors will never lose money, but conditions like last year can test even that guarantee.

Nonetheless, a focus on liquidity and safety puts Black women one step closer to realizing our money-related goals of having financial resources for our families today and for generations to come. What will really anchor us during any financial storm, however, is a biblical view of stewardship that embraces Jesus as our true "safe harbor." While the winds of recession blow, we can be comforted knowing our safe harbor is *"the same yesterday and today and forever"* (Hebrews 13:8). Like our ancestral sisters, we can know that He *will* provide for us; thus, we can trust in Him. As we trust God, we will be more apt to obey the Word of God, follow the leading of the Holy Spirit, and meet the needs of our families and others around us—despite all economic conditions.

REFERENCES

Bridgforth, G. 2000. *Girl, Get Your Money Straight!* New York: Broadway Books.

Hummel, C. 1994. *Tyranny of the Urgent.* Revised and Expanded Edition. Downers Grove, Illinois: InterVarsity Press.

Hunt, M. 2008. *The Financially Confident Woman: The Least Every Woman Needs to Know to Manage Her Finances and Prepare for the Future.* Revised and Expanded Edition. Los Angeles: DPL Press.

Klontz, T., R. Kahler, B. Klontz. 2006. *The Financial Wisdom of Ebenezer Scrooge.* Deerfield Beach, Florida: Health Communications, Inc.

Whitehead, B. 2007. *Why Smart People Do Stupid Things with Money.* New York: Sterling Publishing.

Chapter Seven

SEXUALITY AND
THE SEASONS OF LIFE

*There is a time for everything, and a
season for every activity under heaven.*

ECCLESIASTES 3:1

Amanda Johnson

If we are to succeed in our Christian walk, it is vital that we understand God's sovereignty, magnificent grace, and impeccable timing! Perhaps you've heard the adage "timing is everything." In fact, the difference between success and failure can depend on our timing. Driving through an intersection too soon or too late can mean a catastrophic consequence. Unfortunately, we are all feeling the effects of poor, ill-timed business decisions on behalf of the banking industry and Wall Street. The bottom line is—timing can make or break a good idea.

David was the ruler of Israel's greatest dynasty because he and his military leaders *"understood the times and knew what Israel should do"* (1 Chronicles 12:32). Of course, the most brilliant timing of all occurred because God knew exactly when He would send Jesus—not too early or not too late but— *"when the time had fully come, God sent his Son"* (Galatians 4:4).

SEASONS OF LIFE

Just as God created seasons in nature, He created seasons in which the tasks and events of our lives are to occur. In the wintertime during subzero temperatures, we know to wear a coat. You don't have to spend countless hours in prayer to determine the season of nature and the appropriate corresponding actions. Likewise, it is possible to anticipate what events and behaviors are appropriate according to the season of life we are in.

For example, I live in Michigan. Imagine what would happen if I decide to plant a vegetable garden in the middle of winter. Let's say that I attempt to do this only to later declare that I am a failure at gardening. You would laugh at me and inquire whether I had considered the *season* of the year! Yet, this is what we do in our lives far too often only to find ourselves in a quandary as to why things haven't worked out well for us.

Furthermore, I believe that we can apply the seasons of life principle to our sexuality. Hopefully, you will find the information discussed in this chapter useful and empowering so that you can make the most of whatever season you may be in at the present time.

MARRIAGE: THE APPROPRIATE TIME
FOR SEXUAL PLEASURE AND FULFILLMENT

Many, many years ago, Lady Alice Hillingdon, the wife of the Second Baron Hillingdon, endured her husband's amorous advances for the sake of the greater collective good. At one time, she allegedly wrote in her journal: "I am happy now that George calls on my bedchamber less frequently than of old. As it is, I now endure but two calls a week, and when I hear his steps outside my door I lie down on my bed, close my eyes, and think of England."[1]

Today, you don't hear many women who view their sexuality in the way that Lady Hillingdon did. On the contrary, we live in a culture that is preoccupied with sex to the point that sex is virtually worshiped. The response of parents, pastors, and Christian lay leaders has been to simply say "No! Wait! Cease and desist!" Subsequently, these commands have come to be synonymous with sex in some Christian circles. Despite the rampant abuse of this gift from God, I believe we need to remember why sex, within the context and confines of Christian marriage, is a gloriously wonderful thing.

Sex Is Wholistic

Yet many in this contemporary culture view sex as a singular act that is strictly for physical pleasure. People mistakenly believe that sex can be engaged in by any two consenting adults, devoid of a lasting commitment. On the other hand, Christianity encourages the profound possibilities of sexuality based on love and commitment—and rightly so. The 1993 Janus Survey[2] on sexuality revealed a connection between satisfaction with sex and those respondents who said they had a connection that was not only physical but spiritual and emotional as well.

As a matter of truth, sexuality and spirituality are intimately connected. God calls the church His bride to illustrate the kind of intimacy He longs for us to share with Him. In fact, *yada,* the Hebrew word for sexual intimacy, literally means "to know," as Adam "knew" Eve (Genesis 4:1 KJV). David used the same word, *yadah,* for God when he said in Psalm 139:1, *"O Lord, you have searched me and you know me."* John Donne, sixteenth-century poet and cleric, passionately declared to the Lord: "except you enthrall me, never shall be free, nor ever chaste, except you ravish me."[3]

The paradox of the Christian's intimate relationship with God requires that in order for us to be free, we must be rescued from the bondage of sin and then recaptured and completely submitted to God! This is something earlier Christians understood.

Sex Is Delightful and Fun

Indeed, sex involves some very intense and profoundly serious and intimate emotions. However, Lady Hillingdon may have been aghast to hear that there is a pleasurable side to loving sexuality. Yet, Solomon would enthusiastically agree that marital sex is something enjoyable and precious to behold. The truth is, sexual pleasure in marriage is far more beautiful than any counterfeit interpretation that our culture offers.

The writer of the Song of Solomon tenderly speaks of Abishag in this unique and poetic book of the Bible. He refers to the object of his affections as "my love," a term that speaks to his intimate and sexual friendship with her (see 1:9; 2:2; 4:7; 5:2; and 6:4). Solomon describes her beauty and his love for her in three ways: physically (4:1–5), emotionally (4:6), and spiritually (4:7).

Without the physiological drive to be intimate, most married couples would slowly drift apart. The physical oneness along with emotional and spiritual agreement combines to encourage married couples to share, unite, and enter the souls of each other in a profound way that distinguishes the intimacy of the relationship from any other.

SEXUALITY AND MARITAL SEASONS

There are a lot of stressors that can hinder our ability to experience the joys and wonder of sex in marriage the way God intended. Situations that we encounter in everyday life, family dynamics, church ministries, employment demands, and raising children, all contribute to our stress. There is a real balancing act that must take place in caring for a husband, kids, elderly parents, and so on. In addition to these, there are challenges that come uniquely to different seasons of life. Throughout all of life's events, in order to enjoy the bliss of married love and sexuality, a great deal of compassion, patience, and understanding is needed on the part of both spouses to achieve and sustain a fulfilling home life that encourages passionate expression.

Young Married Couples with Children

During the early season of marriage, our passions make us come alive! It is understandable when newlyweds feel a special obligation to fulfill the intention of Deuteronomy 24:5: *"If a man has recently married, he must not be sent to war or have any other duty laid on him. For one year he is to be free to stay at home and bring happiness to the wife he has married."*

When couples are newly married, both partners are to be captivated by their mutual appreciation of each other. It is a very exclusive season for them. However, when you add a baby carriage to that union, things tend to change drastically. A baby needs constant and undivided attention. The past freedom of sexual expression has to be worked around midnight feedings and fretful cries. An exhausted mom who may be struggling with fluctuating hormones may have a difficult time for a while until she adjusts to caring for her newborn baby. When I encourage young mothers with little children, one of my favorite verses in the Bible is: *"do not despise the day of small things"* (Zechariah 4:10). Admittedly, I use this verse somewhat out of context, but with the best of intentions. I want to emphasize the fact that little children grow up fast. Enjoy the season!

Commandeering the challenges of child rearing so that they do not impinge unduly on the health and vitality of married life continues until children leave home! However, children can be encouraged and taught to honor their parents' relationship and privacy as they grow up and become more independent.

I'd like to remind you that you do not have a covenant love relationship with your children. This unique promise only exists between you and your husband. The health of your marriage should always be your first priority.

Intimacy and the Married Couple: Just Do It!

For married couples only, the message is: Just Do It! By that, I mean, enjoy the intimacies that God intended for husband and wife. I'd like to encourage my married sisters: Don't wait until all of the "i's" are dotted and "t's" crossed and all the "situations" in your life and marriage are resolved to perfection, sorted, or grown up. Just Do It!

There are times during certain seasons where our sexuality may become a spiritual discipline. Ladies, allow me to let you in on a little secret. This one is just for you: you may have to minister to your husband at times when you don't particularly feel compelled to do so. The good news is that both you and your husband always have the invaluable Word of God to gain counsel on this matter: *"The wife's body does not belong to her alone but also to her husband. In the same way, the husband's body does not belong to him alone but also to his wife. Do not deprive each other except by mutual consent and for a time, so that you may devote yourselves to prayer. Then come together again so that Satan will not tempt you because of your lack of self-control"* (1 Corinthians 7:4–5).

It is important to understand that God made human beings with three dimensions: body, soul, and spirit. He is very intentional and everything He does is purposeful. He wants us to appreciate the fact that our physical bodies include the capacity to experience some rather amazing sensations. I can't say this is scriptural, but to further illustrate the importance of sexual pleasure and knowing that God wanted women, in particular, to enjoy the experience, I'd like to think that God gave women a clitoris to make up for the fact that we would frequently have to "keep up" with our husbands in terms of desire and frequency for sex. The male sex organ has multiple physiological functions, but the female clitoris serves only one purpose—sexual pleasure! By design, God gave this special gift to us for no other purpose than to provide women with sexual ecstasy. This was God's idea and God called every aspect of His creation "very good" (Genesis 1:31).

Once you are just "doing it," you will experience the power of marital sex and its overwhelming ability to improve, bind, and heal your relationship.

THE CHALLENGES OF MIDLIFE FOR
WOMEN: THE SEASON OF MENOPAUSE

The midlife season for many women is a time when we experience a new-found freedom in our sexuality. The concern about pregnancy is no longer an issue. And there are no small children in the home that need to be "worked around" to manage private time with your husband. When children have moved on to develop their own lives and interests, this can be a wonderful time to refocus your attentions on pleasing your husband.

On the other hand, the menopausal season can be particularly challenging for some women. The following excerpt is from an e-mail that was posted at the Christian Sex and Marriage blog, http://www.achristiansexsite.com.

First of all, most women know that your body does not respond the same to stimulation. You do not really ever think about sex or ever have any sort of desire for it. Your breasts, clitoris, and vagina become much less sensitive, so the initial stimulation of just being touched has little or no effect on your mental or physical ability to respond. Your body also does not lubricate, therefore without the use of K-Y or another substitute, sex is dry and very painful. It can also cause little tears that will make you have a pink discharge either during or shortly after intercourse. There are a lot of over the counter lubes, and K-Y just keeps coming out with more.

Another thing about the years leading into menopause, known as peri-menopause, is that your period becomes completely unpredictable. This is not only annoying just on terms of life in general, but it puts a re-ally strange twist on your sex life.

There should be a lot more information out there that prepares you for the sexual effects of menopause, because it is something that women tend to just endure alone. Menopause is something that every couple needs to work through together. Women need to be aware of what is happening to their bodies and talk about it, not ignore or hide it or pretend it isn't happening. And men need to help us out by being supportive and loving and by helping us adapt.

This writer mentions most of the complaints that women experience during menopause that adversely affect the ability to relate to their husbands during this season of life. There are medical and herbal remedies that you can use to help address and relieve these problems. If you are experiencing any of these symptoms, please consult your gynecologist.

SEXUALITY: SEASONS OF DIVORCE AND PROLONGED SINGLENESS

This next section is especially challenging for me because I am divorced and have been single for more than fifteen years. As I write this, I struggle with the desire to be cherished and especially loved. I have said frequently to my adult daughters and close friends, a circle that I invite you into now, that I want to be at the top of someone's list. You know, as a mother, I consider the needs and desires of my children. They are at the top of my list. In a marriage relationship, a husband thinks of his wife, and a wife considers her husband. But, as a single mother, where does that leave me?

I have some pretty thoughtful daughters. All five of them are attentive and sensitive to my feelings. But not unlike any healthy parent, I understand that they have their own lives—careers, school, and friends. One of my daughters is married with her own husband and family. Suffice it to say, if you are single and would prefer to be married, I know your pain.

The Truth about Celibacy and Abstinence

If we remove the pat answers that the church gives in regard to those who yearn for physical, emotional, and sexual fulfillment, we have to face some harsh realities:

- The desire for sex does exist; it never goes away completely. Because in addition to God creating us to be spiritual beings, we were also created with physical and emotional as well as sexual needs and desires.
- Until fulfilled, these needs will remain, in some form, a very real need and void.
- For godly single Christians, the physical and sexual yearnings for intimacy that cannot be fulfilled are extremely frustrating (1 Corinthians 7:9).

❋ A little encouragement from the church that says, in effect, "It's difficult and frustrating for you, no doubt, but hang in there! You're doing
the right thing," could go a long way.

For His single daughters, I am obliged to share what God has instructed
us to do. Hopefully, you and I will give our desire for sexual intimacy to God
and see it as a unique opportunity to return our love to Him who first loved
us. We must choose deprivation rather than depravity. And that choice becomes
our love offering to Christ. And know that we will never be disappointed.

Let's look at Genesis 29:20 to consider Jacob's state of mind: *"So Jacob
served seven years to get Rachel, but they seemed like only a few days to him because of his love for her."* Time was relative to Jacob, and so it must be for you
and me. This is how I look at it: If I'm too old to swing from the chandelier,
at least I'll be able to hit the light switch!

Can You (and I) Be Lonely, but Happy?

Frequently, I hear single people say, "I'll be happy when I get married," or
"I'll be happy when I have children," or "I'll be happy when I can have sex
again." All of these statements have the direct implication that our happiness
is contingent on another state of being, namely, the absence of loneliness. We
make our ability to be happy conditional. We can only be happy when everything is "perfect"—when our most desired state becomes a reality and loneliness is cast into the abyss of no more. This is a dangerous philosophy to
espouse because the tendency is to postpone the possibility of enjoying many
other facets and joys of life. I've even heard people say they were not going to
purchase their first home or take a special vacation until they got married.

The Tyranny of the Calendar

God is the God of eternity. I once heard a pastor say that he recognizes this
fact but he had to remind God that, even though God is in no particular hurry
to address His concerns with us, the pastor acknowledged that he doesn't have
that long. I've come to own this phrase because I understand what he is saying. So, God, would it be possible for You to speed things up a bit? To that I
say, "Amen."

I would like to get married while I am still kind of young. Actually, I'm middle-aged and enjoying my life very much since I can still swing from a chandelier or two. However, I strenuously object to the notion of putting any pursuit or adventure on hold, waiting for "him" to come and sweep me off my feet. I sincerely hope that you will not wait for loneliness to disappear from your landscape in order to experience and enjoy all the other blessings God has for you.

DISCOVER AND FULFILL
GOD'S PURPOSE FOR YOUR LIFE

It was in the course of her normal, daily routine that Rachel was discovered by Jacob. Rachel did not waste her time peering into a pool of water at her reflection, daydreaming about a speculative suitor. Nor did she put her life on hold until one appeared. Rachel was busy doing the work set before her. She was attending to her responsibilities and wisely made "the most of every opportunity" (Ephesians 5:15–16). Rachel had a strategy for success in her singleness and she was rewarded for how she conducted her life. Listen to the account in Genesis 29;1–13 of her meeting with Jacob for the first time:

Then Jacob continued on his journey and came to the land of the eastern peoples. There he saw a well in the field, with three flocks of sheep lying near it because the flocks were watered from that well. The stone over the mouth of the well was large. When all the flocks were gathered there, the shepherds would roll the stone away from the well's mouth and water the sheep. Then they would return the stone to its place over the mouth of the well.

Jacob asked the shepherds, "My brothers, where are you from?" "We're from Haran," they replied.

He said to them, "Do you know Laban, Nahor's grandson?" "Yes, we know him," they answered.

Then Jacob asked them, "Is he well?"

"Yes, he is," they said, "and here comes his daughter Rachel with the sheep."

"Look," he said, "the sun is still high; it is not time for the flocks to be gathered. Water the sheep and take them back to pasture."

"We can't," they replied, "until all the flocks are gathered and the stone has been rolled away from the mouth of the well. Then we will water the sheep."

While he was still talking with them, Rachel came with her father's sheep, for she was a shepherdess. When Jacob saw Rachel daughter of Laban, his mother's brother, and Laban's sheep, he went over and rolled the stone away from the mouth of the well and watered his uncle's sheep. Then Jacob kissed Rachel and began to weep aloud. He had told Rachel that he was a relative of her father and a son of Rebekah. So she ran and told her father. As soon as Laban heard the news about Jacob, his sister's son, he hurried to meet him. He embraced him and kissed him and brought him to his home, and there Jacob told him all these things.

Notice that when Jacob saw Rachel, he was clearly taken by her. He knew that their meeting each other was God's doing. Therefore, he *knew* she was *the one.* Perhaps that's why he was so overcome with emotion as he wept and kissed Rachel. He had to wait on God just as you and I are waiting. Perhaps those tears were full of relief and gratitude that he had finally found her.

Like Rachel, singles must diligently pursue and perfect their gifts and talents. We are to use them to pursue the vocation and ministry that God has planned uniquely for each one of us. The scope and sequence of our training is outlined by the apostle Peter: *"Giving all diligence, add to your faith virtue; and to virtue knowledge; and to knowledge temperance; and to temperance patience; and to patience godliness; and to godliness brotherly kindness; and to brotherly kindness charity"* (2 Peter 1:5–7 KJV).

The Reality of Loneliness

At this juncture, I want to remind all of us that marriage is not a guaranteed cure for the ailment of loneliness. There are scores of married people who are still looking for companionship and understanding that their spouse does not provide. The reality is that loneliness is a fact of life. The life of Jesus bears this out. He was the most together person to ever walk the earth, yet His experience included times of deep and profound loneliness. I believe this is a longing that can only be satisfied by God, who truly is the perfect lover of our souls and the singular personality who can totally satisfy our desire for oneness and exclusivity.

What Role Will Loneliness Play in Your Life?

If we can agree that loneliness is a fact of life, what can we do about it? I think we can decide that loneliness will not be the overarching theme of our lives; we can refuse to allow loneliness to be the dominant force that drives us. The only way we will succeed in our determination to make this happen is if we rely on the Holy Spirit for help. We frequently forget that He is the presence of God on earth, living inside us to give us encouragement and guidance. When we allow Him to be the Lover of our souls and in charge of our outlook, attitudes, and perspective, we can be happy people who know occasional times of loneliness, instead of lonely people who know occasional times of happiness. This is an important distinction that is more than just a play on words—it's truly an achievable goal.

CONCLUSION

I chuckle at myself. In the summer, I complain about the heat. In the winter, it's too cold. I think my tendency to wish for the summer in winter and winter in summer can serve as a commentary on humanity. No matter where we find ourselves, the grass is always greener on the other side. The next place always holds more promise than the current locale.

This summer I am going to enjoy wearing short sleeves, working in my garden, sitting in the shade, and drinking lemonade. I will appreciate the virtues of central air-conditioning instead of complaining about the heat. I beseech you to enjoy the benefits of your current season too. Don't despise it! Another follows with its own unique gifts and challenges.

REFERENCES

1. The phrase "lie back and think of England," used in the United Kingdom during the Victorian Era is likened to the sayings "grit your teeth," or "grin and bear it." The origins of the phrase are unclear but it is generally attributed to Lady Alice Hillingdon (1857–1940).

2. A survey of 2,765 people (1,347 men and 1,418 women) done from 1988–1992 was conducted using anonymously completed questionnaires and 125 in-depth interviews. Originally, 4,550 questionnaires were distributed across the country. There was a return rate of 61 percent that represented a typical cross section of respondents using characteristics such as gender, age, income, and education. The Januses had a team of researchers spanning the forty-eight contiguous states. The Janus Report resulted in a book published in 1993, *The Janus Report on Sexual Behavior.*

3. Excerpt from "Batter My Heart," John Donne (1573–1631), Holy Sonnet XIV.

SUGGESTED READINGS

Brown, D. 2008. *Just Do It: How One Couple Turned Off the TV and Turned On Their Sex Lives for 101 Days (No Excuses!).*New York: Crown Publishers.

Christian Sex and Marriage blog, http://www.achristiansexsite.com.

Ford, J. 2004. *When a Man Loves a Woman.* Chicago, Illinois: Moody Publishers.

Hocking, C., and D. Hocking. 1986. *Romantic Lovers: The Intimate Marriage.* Eugene, Oregon: Harvest House.

Lewis, C. S. 1991. *The Four Loves.* Orlando, Florida: Harcourt Brace.

Chapter Eight

THE SOJOURN OF SINGLES:
DECISION AT THE CROSSROAD

Cross

\kros\ *noun*
A structure or monument
consisting of an upright and
a transverse piece upon
which Jesus died. A symbol
of Christianity for those who
accept it.

Crossroad

\kros'rōd'/ *noun*
A point at which a vital
decision must be made.
The place where roads
intersect.
A main center of activity.

Road

\rōd\ *noun*
A paved surface made
for traveling.

Valerie Clayton

A Decision Point

Crossroads in life are good because they force us to make choices that can change our direction. I was twenty-nine years old when I hit a major crossroad in my life. That was when I realized that I would not achieve my goal of being married by age thirty. I had just broken up with the boyfriend who brought out the worst parts of my personality. Instead of rejoicing over my newfound freedom, I was heartbroken. And it wasn't because we were no longer a couple. I was devastated because I knew that 180 days would not be sufficient time to meet, date, and marry my yet-to-be-found husband. So, instead of immediately resuming my search like I had done in the past—I sank into despair. I had always thought that marriage would have been a natural life step. But, like most Black women, meeting and marrying my Prince Charming proved to be elusive. I was at a crossroad. I had to take a hard look at my life.

When I was in college, dating was relatively easy. There were Black Student Union dances, frat parties, and blind dates. We met men everywhere: walking in the mall, at the park, attending a game, in the library, and even on the freeway. For me, college and my early twenties was a big social whirlwind. My girls and I (of course, we traveled in packs back then) were looking for tall, muscular, moody men—the ones with smoldering eyes, a quick wit, and a sports car. These edgy, dangerous, manly men were, of course, not the marrying kind.

That wasn't uppermost in our minds. We wanted to have fun: travel to exotic islands, build our careers through strategic chesslike moves, stretch our wings, and have many adventures. So, I attempted to soar through life without a thought for my future. But, like Icarus, who flew too close to the sun with wings of feathers and wax, I too plunged back to earth and reality. When I woke up, I realized that I wanted to get married and there were no marriageable men in sight.

In the beginning, *"the Lord God said, 'It is not good for the man to be alone'"* (Genesis 2:18). Far too many Black women end up just like that—alone. There are approximately 36.4 million African Americans comprising about 12.9 percent of the population living in the United States.[1] According to Marital Status 2000, a U.S. Census brief, only 31 percent of Black women were married at the time the 2000 Census was taken.[2] In fact, Black men and women had the lowest marital percentages of any race at 42 percent for Black men, and just 31 percent for Black women.[3] On the other hand, Asians had one of the highest marital percentages: 60 percent for men and 61 percent for women.[4] Blacks also had the highest percentage of any racial group for the category of never married: 39.7 percent of Black women have never been married compared to 20.8 percent of White women; 41.6 percent Black men compared to 27.3 percent of White men.[5]

THE POSTPONEMENT OF MARRIAGE

My mother was a widow. She married my father when she was 25. I was born when she was 28, my sister was born when she turned 30, and Mother buried her husband by 36. One of the things she had always stressed to my sister and I was to get our education because we may have to support ourselves.

According to the National Marriage Project at Rutgers, the number one reason given for the postponement of marriage was to become financially stable.[6] Since 1970, marriage has been delayed. I speculate that perhaps there is a significant correlation in the increasing percentage of never-married adults in the United States. In 1970, 36 percent of women between the ages of 20–24 were never married; however, by 2003 that percentage had soared to 75 percent.[7]

The changes were just as drastic for men. In 1970, the proportion of men who were never married for ages 20–24 increased from 55 percent in 1970 to

86 percent in 2003.[8] In 1970, the average age for first marriage was 20.8 years old for women and 23.2 for men.[9] By 2003, the average age for women increased to 25.3 years and for men 27.1.[10] However, research writer Andrew J. Cherlin reports that when we look back to the 1950s, nearly all young adults married: approximately 95 percent of Whites and 88 percent of Blacks.[11]

Historically, not only have Blacks married, but we did our best to maintain a two-parent household. New York historian Herbert G. Gutman proposed in his book *The Black Family in Slavery and Freedom, 1750–1925* that the two-parent household and long-lasting marriages were "typical" among Blacks. His supposition was supported by the analysis of slave registers and Reconstruction Period marriage records. In "Black Families: Surviving Slavery," *Time* magazine reports: "Gutman's conclusion: from the earliest days of slavery until the eve of the Great Depression, the black family was surprisingly close, strong and intact."[12]

However, James Q. Wilson (2002) notes in his book *The Marriage Problem* that Gutman's findings have been challenged in that he focused on slave records of large plantations where, it has been argued, maintaining an intact family was easier because of fewer sales. The majority of slave owners had small plantations or farms and the maintenance of an intact Black family was not the priority and did not occur.[13]

WHY WON'T MEN COMMIT?

For decades, women have wondered why men won't commit. However, in the past twenty years, the foot-dragging of men has become much more pronounced. The National Marriage Project, a nonpartisan, nonsectarian, and interdisciplinary initiative located at Rutgers, the State University of New Jersey, has attempted to answer that very question. The mission of the Marriage Project includes providing "research and analysis on the state of marriage in America and to educate the public on the social, economic and cultural conditions affecting marital success and well-being."[14] In 2002, the National Marriage Project published a study entitled "Why Men Won't Commit: Exploring Young Men's Attitudes about Sex, Dating and Marriage." The top two reasons men have no incentive to establish lifelong relationships with women are:

1. They can get sex without marriage more easily than in times past, and

2. They can enjoy the benefits of having a wife by cohabiting rather than marrying.[15]

> The men in this study express a desire to marry and have children sometime in their lives, but they are in no hurry. They enjoy their single life and they experience few of the traditional pressures from church, employers or the society that once encouraged men to marry. Moreover, the sexual revolution and the trend toward cohabitation offer them some of the benefits without its obligations. If this trend continues, it will not be good news for the many young women who hope to marry and bear children before they begin to face problems associated with declining fertility.[16]

The study cited ten reasons why men won't commit. However, women allowing men to enjoy the benefits of uncommitted sex are at the root of why there are such high percentages of Black men who have never married. Sex without the benefit of marital commitment not only leads to prolonged singleness for women, but it is the primary cause of Black children being born out of wedlock. More than 66 percent of Black births in 2005 were to unmarried women.[17] In the states of Mississippi and Louisiana, the unmarried Black birth rate has soared to 77 percent.[18]

The study continues with the exploration of a man's feelings about a woman with whom he has had sex:

> Once they have casual sex, men say, they are less respectful and interested in pursuing a relationship with a woman. "If a girl wants it on the first night we go out, I definitely lose respect for her, 'cause she's probably doing it with someone else." They are more likely to "take it slow" sexually when they are romantically interested in a woman.[19]

Men won't commit because there is no reason for them to make a commitment when they can get sex without one. Some of the other reasons cited by men for delaying marriage included being able to retain financial resources, wanting to own a home, wanting to delay having children, and the enjoyment of dating many women.[20]

WHAT SHOULD WE DO?

Black women have always faced challenges. In generations past, we faced the challenge of being captured to endure the Middle Passage, only to be enslaved and sold. We have been whipped, raped, and worked. We have borne children under these less-than-favorable conditions, fought for our freedom, and searched for family. Generations later, we marched, voted, looked for jobs, scrimped, saved, and made better lives for our children. Every generation has had its own challenges and dark times.

In this generation, *one* of the challenges we are faced with is a lack of marriageable Black men. So, what is a woman to do when she wants to share her life with someone special and there is no one on the horizon? What does a woman do when she desires to date and has not been asked out—in years? None of us are accidents, regardless of the circumstances of our birth. God specifically and purposefully created each of us to exist right now—in this season. Therefore we, like Esther, must realize that our lives were positioned *"for such a time as this"* (Esther 4:14).

There is no magic formula about what to do as a single woman. However, I do think we see one significant thing in the lives of Jacob and Rachel: **she was busy doing the work God had given her**—serving her family by watering the animals—when Jacob found her at the well! *"Rachel came with her father's sheep, for she was a shepherdess. When Jacob saw Rachel daughter of Laban, his mother's brother, and Laban's sheep, he went over and rolled the stone away from the mouth of the well and watered his uncle's sheep"* (Genesis 29:9–10). Rachel had the right idea; we cannot go wrong when we focus our time and energy on doing whatever God has placed in our hands to do.

Besides that, formulas don't work because every individual is unique. To put it simply, we are in a battle. The Enemy's objective is to steal your hope. But be reminded that hoping in God does not disappoint the one who does not give up (Romans 5:5)—so hold on to it with all of your might. Without hope, there is no future.

One could say that Viktor Frankl is an expert on hope. His book *Man's Search for Meaning*,[21] is a landmark work that was birthed out of Dr. Frankl's personal experience and the observations he made while being held as a prisoner in various Nazi concentration camps. He stated in his book that once hope had been lost, a person died shortly thereafter:

The prisoner who had lost faith in the future—his future—was doomed. With his loss of belief in the future, he also lost his spiritual hold; he let himself decline and became subject to mental and physical decay. Usually this happened quite suddenly, in the form of a crisis.

The circumstances facing Black women are harsh. The news is not good. But, knowing that *"for **nothing** is impossible with God"* (Luke 1:37, emphasis mine) keeps us looking to Him with the assurance that He will not let us down. With that in mind, the following are suggestions that have made a difference for me and helped me to maintain my hope in God and the possibility of marriage in my life.

Choose to Believe God

God gave us the ability to choose. We can choose to believe Him or we can choose to believe our circumstances. We can believe His promises or we can listen to the world tell us it's impossible. Remember when Moses sent the twelve spies to scout out the Promised Land (Numbers 13)? He told them to find out about the land and discover whether the people who inhabited it were strong or weak. All of the spies agreed that the land was good and flowed with milk and honey (Numbers 13:27). Ten of the spies reported that the people of the land were stronger than they were (Numbers 13:31–33).

But Caleb and Joshua said, *"if the Lord is pleased with us . . . he will give it to us . . . do not be afraid . . . "* (from Numbers 14:8–9). Unfortunately, the people of Israel chose to fear; and, as a result, that generation never made it to the Promised Land (Numbers 14:20–24). Their children, however, chose to believe God and forty years later (after all of the unbelievers died off) God gave them the land He had promised!

Choosing to believe God is a life crossroad. In those dark moments of doubt—wondering if God hears or will answer your prayer—you are at a decision point. Is doubt, in itself, wrong? No, because doubt forces us to examine our lives and dig into God's Word. Doubt drives us to our knees in prayer and forces us to make a decision. The Bible says in Deuteronomy 30:19, *"This day I call heaven and earth as witnesses against you that I have set before you life and death, blessings and curses. Now **choose life**, so that you and your children may live"* (emphasis mine).

Choose Life!

How do you choose God when you have doubt, when you're uncertain, hesitant to believe, and when you're fearful? In other words, *how* do you choose life? First, understand that to doubt is part of being human. It is part of the pathway we must take to embrace God: we must confront our doubts. Second, know that when you are in doubt, according to James 1:2–3, we are to *"consider it pure joy . . . whenever you face trials of many kinds, because you know that the testing of your faith develops perseverance."* The very act of wrestling to overcome doubt is proof that your faith is being tested. God tells us that we should consider this fight against fear and doubt as something that can produce joy. Why? **Because the purpose of this type of testing is to develop spiritual strength, endurance, and perseverance.** When we wrestle with our doubts and choose to believe God's Word in spite of our circumstances, we gain strength. WELL SAID!

When It Is Dark, Walk by Faith

God designed us to walk by faith. In order for us to hold His hand in the dark times of our lives, we must have hope that His hand is, in fact, there for us. Hope helps us to walk by faith. It is when our hope is tested that our character is being shaped. It is God's desire that when dark times of the soul occur—we draw closer to Him. It is in those times of closeness that He reveals to us His purpose for our lives and gives meaning to our suffering. Ultimately, God teaches us the total freedom of leaning on Him whether our circumstances change or not.

Well, how do we know that we have any faith? Because God gives it to us. The Word says that God gives each of us a *"measure of faith"* (Romans 12:3). All of us receive the amount that is sufficient and appropriate for our current situation. Strong faith comes from arriving at different life crossroads and choosing to believe God's Word for one more moment. All we have to do is choose to believe God right now—in this moment—this very instant. Don't concern yourself about believing for tomorrow, or next week, or next year. Only concern yourself with what you believe about God this very second. Choose to believe that God desires to bless you. Choose to believe that all things work together for the good of those who love Him. Choose to believe that God is for you and not against you. The choice is yours.

Ignore the Statistics

Statistics can be scary. Statistics are menacing, especially when you measure your desires against probability. There was a statistic that frightened me many years ago; it was featured in the now infamous cover article "The Marriage Crunch" that ran in *Newsweek* magazine in June 1986.[22] Basically, *Newsweek* reported that a White, college-educated woman who was single by age 40 had a better chance of being killed by a terrorist than getting married based on a 2.6 chance of probability. This article was written fourteen years before 9/11 occurred, so can you imagine what an uproar it caused? We had never experienced a terrorist attack on U.S. soil. Subsequently, that statistic has been proven to be radically false.[23] However, it caused great fear in single women at the time.

Statistics can cause us to doubt God. But, regardless of what statisticians say about Black marriage rates—choose to believe God. One of the things I do is flip statistics around. For instance, if 41.6 percent of Black men have never been married,[24] then I say, wow. That sounds pretty good to me because God only needs to touch the heart of *one* man if I am believing God for a husband.

Also, realize that, when we are in Christ, God brings love to us in many packages. The man that God may have for you may not be African American. We believers are part of one body; all of us are in Christ (1 Corinthians 12:13). Keep your mind and your heart open to all possibilities and don't put limitations on what God can do for you.

DO YOU LIKE MEN?

If you want to marry a man, you have to first like men. Do you enjoy their company? Do you feel comfortable with having male friends? Do they make you laugh? Do you "get" how they think? Do you appreciate the differences between men and women in terms of our natures?

Because I grew up in an all-female household (even our dog was female), I had very limited contact with the male sex. I didn't talk to them or understand them. I just knew that I needed one if I wanted to get married. While in college, even though I dated them, men were still foreign creatures to me. It wasn't until I arrived at yet another crossroad that I decided that I really needed to get to know men on a friend-to-friend basis. That's when I started making true lifelong friendships with men. I met the majority of my male friends at church, along with a sprinkle from work. We would laugh, talk, and do things together—as friends. If one of us needed an escort to an event, we were there for each other.

Men make wonderful friends. They are funny, sometimes blunt, and can be a breath of fresh air. You can get a different opinion about life, a clarity about situations that sometimes women lack. Make the extra effort to make a male friend. It's worth it.

Smile

One thing I kept hearing from men is that Black women can be intimidating. How was I intimidating? I was friendly—I thought. Fairly outgoing—I presumed. Finally, my stepfather (my mom married a wonderful man in her fifties) gave me the key that I needed to break down the intimidation barrier. He said that Black women don't smile at men and we walk too fast. He went on to say that no man could catch up to me even if he did want to say something! So, I took his advice; I slowed my roll and started smiling at men. Not just the ones that appeared eligible but all men of any color, young or old. It didn't matter.

I started talking to men everywhere: in elevators, on the street, in the row in front of me at church. Since I wanted to marry a believer, I would always make sure that I looked extra nice for church and then greeted as many men as possible. I not only acknowledged the cuties but the halt, the lame, and the odd ones too. I discovered that marriageable men watch who women show kindness to, then they form an overall opinion about those women. Demonstrate genuine kindness to those around you. And it all starts with a smile. Scripture says, *"A man who has friends must himself be friendly"* (Proverbs 18:24).

Angry? Forgive and Move On

Who has hurt you? All of us have been hurt in life whether from a past relationship, a family mess, or even being angry at yourself for poor choices. Your beef may be legitimate and your anger justified. However, with that said, there is a fine line between justified anger and bitterness. Bitterness is the intense feeling of resentment that arises out of an event that is perceived to be an injustice. Not only is bitterness a feeling, but it is also a process. It is the gradual turning cold of our once warm hearts. The results of bitterness are seen in the withdrawing of love, the turning away from others, the protective walls we build around our hearts, and the unwillingness to trust. [25]

There is only one way you can get rid of bitterness, and that is by forgiving. Forgiveness is a decision—not a feeling. Forgiveness is not based on the actions of the other person. We forgive to set *ourselves* free from bitterness. The act of forgiveness is a burden-lifting choice that you can make for your well-being and your future.

Embrace Celibacy

James Q. Wilson, in his article entitled "Why We Don't Marry," stated, "The sexual revolution was supposed to make men and women equal. Instead it has helped men, while leaving many women unmarried spectators watching *Sex and the City.* "[26] Study after study confirms the fact that sex outside of marriage never benefits the woman. If a man is going to leave you because you won't give him sex, he's going to leave you anyway after you do give him sex.

To me, the best thing about celibacy was that it separated the men who were serious about me from those who were hit-and-run artists in disguise. On the first date or no later than the second, I told every man I dated that I was celibate. I got dumped—a lot. Yes, I shed a few tears, but ultimately I was thankful to find out the type of man that I had on my hands. Celibacy keeps you from wasting time in a relationship that wasn't going to work out anyway.

God's Word tells us in 1 Corinthians 6:18–20 to *"Flee from sexual immorality. All other sins a man commits are outside his body, but he who sins sexually sins against his own body. Do you not know that your body is a temple of the Holy Spirit, who is in you, whom you have received from God? You are not your own; you were bought at a price. Therefore honor God with your body."*

God is the one who created sex. He is not telling you to flee sexual immorality because He is a killjoy. He's trying to prevent you from getting hurt: spiritually, emotionally, and physically. This admonition is critical for Black women in today's dangerous health environment.

A MATTER OF LIFE AND DEATH

AIDS is now the number one killer of Black women between the ages of 25–34 and the second-leading cause of death in Black men ages 35–44.[27] In Washington, DC, more than 80 percent of new HIV cases are among Blacks.[28] As stated in the article entitled "Black Women's Burden: An Epidemic of HIV": "Black men had an HIV incidence rate that was six times that of white men in 2006, according to the new CDC report."[29] This statistic is supported by the findings of Dr. Kevin Fenton, Director of the Centers for Disease Control for HIV/AIDS, who states: "The HIV incidence rate for black men was 115.7 per 100,000, compared with 19.6 among white men and 43.1 among Hispanics."

Further, more and more Black women are contracting HIV through heterosexual relations. It has always been wise to practice celibacy, which is an exercise in how much we trust God. What every single woman needs to understand is that celibacy was not designed to hurt you; rather, it is to give you clarity—not only spiritually—but in how you view your relationships too.

GIVE OF YOURSELF

You were born for such a time as this! God gave gifts and experiences to you that He gave to no one else on earth. You can make a difference in your neighborhood, at work, or in your church. Encourage a child. Befriend a senior. Welcome a stranger. Use your imagination.

One of the most exciting things I did was to volunteer after work at one of the major trauma centers in the city. Everything came through those doors: heart attacks, gunshot wounds, assaults, burn victims, stabbings, the mentally ill, those about to give birth, and the like. It was sobering to see life and death unfold before my eyes, but it gave me an opportunity to intercede for others at a critical juncture in their lives. Many nights I would come home bone-tired, but it was so worth it.

So, my advice to you is, bloom where you're planted. You can make where you are a more beautiful place.

ONE ORDINARY SUNDAY

As Jewel Diamond Taylor once said, "Nothing smells worse than the fragrance of desperation." By applying the very things I have shared, my life became more meaningful, fun, and attractive. I did end up getting married—to a man at my church who later shared that he had watched me for two years. Why did he wait so long? Because he didn't think that I would date him since he is six years younger than me. What encouraged him to make his first move? I inadvertently befriended his best friend.

One ordinary Sunday, I prayed with a woman who was discouraged about being single and I shared with her what was working for me. Later that week, I called her to see how she was doing and I invited her to my home to join my friends and me. It turned out that she was *his* best friend. She was the one who encouraged *him* to make that first move—and he did. He told her to tell me that there was someone at church "who thinks she's the bomb!" Three days later, he sent a dozen roses to my job with a card that read, "From the one you've heard about who thinks you're so fine."

For thirty days he showered me with poetry, cards, and letters describing his personality and his relationship with Christ. Lastly, he had an invitation for dinner delivered to me so that we could meet face-to-face. When I walked into the restaurant to meet my secret admirer, it turned out to be a man I had greeted many times at church over the years. By the way, he beat me to the celibacy talk. He informed me that same night that he was celibate and intended to remain that way until his wedding night. From that first date until today, we've been together. We dated for nine months and then he proposed. We were married a year later.

CONCLUSION

We will all face many crossroads that will cause us to examine our lives and revisit some choices. Choose to walk with God. Be fully assured that He sees you and loves you. Harriet Tubman said it best: "Lord, I'm going to hold steady on to You and You've got to see me through."

Beloved, God will see you through. *"May God himself, the God of peace, sanctify you through and through. May your whole spirit, soul and body be kept blameless at the coming of our Lord Jesus Christ. The one who calls you is faithful and he will do it"* (1 Thessalonians 5:23–24). To this, we humbly and joyfully say:

> *I will praise you, O Lord, among the nations;*
> *I will sing of you among the peoples.*
> *For great is your love, reaching to the heavens;*
> *Your faithfulness reaches to the skies.*
> *Be exalted, O God, above the heavens;*
> *Let your glory be over all the earth.*
> —PSALM 57:9–11

REFERENCES

1. Census 2000 Brief. *The Black Population 2000.* Issued August 2001. U.S. Department of Commerce, Economics and Statistics Administration. U.S. Census Bureau.

2. Census 2000 Brief. *Marital Status 2000.* Issued October 2003. U.S. Department of Commerce. Economics and Statistics Administration. U.S. Census Bureau.

3. Ibid., 4. The Black male marriage rate is higher because Black men are more likely than Black women to marry a nonBlack person.

4. Ibid., 4.

5. Ibid., 3. Located on Table 1—Marital Status of the Population Aged 15 and Over by Sex, Age, Race and Hispanic Origin: 2000.

6. Popenoe, David. *Why Men Won't Commit: Exploring Young Men's Attitudes About Sex, Dating and Marriage;* The State of Our Unions 2002; The National Marriage Project. Rutgers, The State University of New Jersey, 15.

7. America's Families and Living Arrangements: 2003. U.S. Census Bureau; U.S. Department of Commerce. Population Characteristics. Issued November 2004.

8. Ibid, 12.

9. Ibid., 12.

10. Ibid., 12.

11. Cherlin, Andrew J. "American marriage in the early twenty-first century." *The Future of Children.* Vol. 15/No.2/Fall 2005. P. 34.

12. *Time* magazine. "Black Families: Surviving Slavery." November 22, 1976 edition. Vol.108 No. 21.

13. Wilson, James Q. "The black family and slavery." *Public Interest Journal.* Spring 2002. Excerpt from the book *The Marriage Problem* by James Q. Wilson. 2002. New York: HarperCollins Publishers.

14. The State of Our Unions 2004. The National Marriage Project. Rutgers, The State University of New Jersey, 2.

15. Popenoe, David. "Why Men Won't Commit: Exploring Young Men's Attitudes About Sex, Dating and Marriage." The State of Our Unions 2002. The National Marriage Project. Rutgers, The State University of New Jersey, 6.

16. Ibid., 6.

17. Popenoe, David. "The Future of Marriage in America." State of Our Unions 2007: The Social Health of Marriage in America, 25.

18. Popenoe, David. *The Red/Blue American Family Divide*; Social Indicators of Marital Health and Wellbeing: Trends of the Past Four Decades. State of Our Unions 2007: The Social Health of Marriage in America, 14.

19. Popenoe, David. "Why Men Won't Commit: Exploring Young Men's Attitudes About Sex, Dating and Marriage." The State of Our Unions 2002. The National Marriage Project. Rutgers, The State University of New Jersey, 10.

20. Ibid., 15.

21. Frankl, Viktor E. (2006 paperback edition). *Man's Search for Meaning.* Boston: Beacon Press.

22. Salholz, Eloise, and Pamela Abramson. "The Marriage Crunch," June 1986 edition. *Newsweek* magazine. "The Marriage Crunch" was based on a study by Harvard and Yale researchers that projected that college-educated women had a 2.6 percent change of getting married if they were still single at 40.

23. Harris, Lynn. "OK Singles, Now You Can Worry About Terrorism." *Newsweek* magazine. May 24, 2006. www.salon.com/mwt/broad

sheet/2006/05/24/newsweek_marriage/print.html.

24. McGinn, Daniel: "Marriage by the Numbers." *Newsweek* magazine. June 5, 2006 edition. http://www.namb.net/atf/cf/%7BCDA250E8-8866-4236-9A0C-C646DE153446%7D/SINGLE.PDF.

25. Clayton, Valerie, and Jerome Clayton. 2002. *Victory in Singleness: A Strategy for Emotional Peace.* Chicago: Moody Publishers. Pg. 141.

26. Wilson, James Q. "Why We Don't Marry." *City Journal.* Winter 2002. http://www.city-journal.org.

27. CNN: *Black in America.* "Black U.S. AIDS Rates Rival Some African Nations."http://www.cnn.com/2008/HEALTH/conditions/07/29/black.aids.report/index.html.

28. Ibid.

29. Payne, Jeffrey W. 2008. "Black Women's Burden: An Epidemic of HIV." *U.S. News and World Report.* http://health.usnews.com/articles/health/2008/09/12/black-womens burden-an-epidemic-of-hiv.html. MedPage Today http://www.medpagetoday.com/HIVAIDS/HIVAIDS/10876.

Chapter Nine

FOR LOVERS ONLY:
THE SANCTITY OF THE
MARRIAGE COVENANT

The Lord God said, "It is not good for the man to be alone. I will make a helper suitable for him" ... The man said, "This is now bone of my bones and flesh of my flesh; she shall be called 'woman,' for she was taken out of man." For this reason a man will leave his father and mother and be united to his wife, and they will become one flesh.

GENESIS 2:18, 23–24

Dr. Doretha O'Quinn

Marriage is the most sacred institution on earth! It is sacred because it is divinely ordained by God. God uniquely compares marriage to His relationship with Christian believers. As a Black woman who has been married to the same man for thirty-five years, I can assure you that, as wonderful as it is, marriage is not without its challenges.

To ensure that your union will last a lifetime, the best strategy to employ is to consult the architect and build on His original design and purposes for marriage. In His Word, God gives us very precise directives regarding how He intends marriage to work. Keep in mind that God honors this sacred institution by comparing it to His relationship with the church: *"Wives, submit yourselves unto your own husbands, as unto the Lord. For the husband is the head of the wife even as Christ is the head of the church"* (Ephesians 5:22 KJV).

There are some biblical principles we must acknowledge and apply that are foundational as they form the cornerstone of successful marital relationships. These include:

1. The Pledge: A Covenant Relationship
2. The Power: Affirmation and Contentment
3. The Precept: Submission in Marriage

THE PLEDGE: A COVENANT RELATIONSHIP

I take thee to be my lawfully wedded spouse, to have and to hold, from this day forward, for better or for worse, for richer or for poorer, in sickness and in health, 'til death do us part, according to God's holy ordinance and thereto I pledge thee my troth.

The language may sound antiquated, but the premise of this promise is as relevant today as it was in the fifteenth century when the tradition of exchanging vows in front of a church official started! However, the significance of these words doesn't really hit home until after the wedding reception and, perhaps, an idyllic honeymoon vacation. Of course, when their vows are uttered, the bride and groom love each other.

But, the implications and full magnitude of the promise is rarely realized until the pressures of contemporary life, along with the traditions, preferences, and philosophies of two families come to bear and begin the blending process. Assuredly, both husband and wife have the best of intentions, with limited perception in regard to the depth of unconditional love and respect required to uphold such a promise. They are engaged with a promise that has not been tested by time and turmoil.

My Story

In 1951, two babies entered the world, one in the month of June, the other in November. One of the children was born in California and the other in Texas. Neither of these children or their parents had any idea that the two would one day meet and would be destined to spend their lives together in marriage. This is how my story began. There were similarities in the way we were raised. Both our families taught us to be strong, loyal, and fun-loving.

However, the ways in which we developed those qualities were unique to each of our families and lifestyles. Little did we know that how we grew up would challenge the foundation of our union more than either of us could ever anticipate. Despite the odds, my husband and I shared a commitment to stay married. That commitment and our mutual relationship with Jesus Christ established the foundation of our marriage and served as an anchor, allowing us to weather each storm that threatened our marital peace.

The vows we exchanged on our wedding day were a covenant with God.

We knew God had brought us together and our meeting was not just a mere coincidence. My husband prayed for a church girl, and I prayed for a loving man. We were convinced that ours would be a sustained, enduring union. We agreed that leaving our marriage could be compared to leaving God, since our marriage covenant included Him! We had no choice but to use the principles in God's Word to deal with any challenges that threatened our relationship. This determination has sustained us—after thirty-five years of marriage we are still a couple.

A COVENANT AGREEMENT VERSUS A CONTRACTUAL AGREEMENT

A covenant has a totally different quality and disposition than a contract. A contract establishes limits of performance and restrictions and presupposes distrust, insincerity, and default, while a covenant establishes permanency and presupposes trust, love, respect, and fidelity. A contract is concerned with "business as usual," conducted expeditiously, while a covenant is concerned with the "heart" of a matter and considers time of no consequence. Furthermore, contracts are "made to be broken"; whereas covenants are eternal and designed to be kept.

In comparison, God establishes a bond of permanent union and communion with every Christian. Three elements make up this special bond we have with Him. They are relevant to our discussion because the same elements are present in the covenant of marriage.

1. Promise and Privilege

When we receive Christ, God promises that He will be our God, we shall be His people, and He will provide eternal life, never leaving or forsaking us (Leviticus 26:12; Jeremiah 24:7; Ezekiel 11:19; John 1:12; Hebrews 13:5). Moreover, the promise of eternal life is not contingent on our behavior. It is a benefit of God's unconditional love for His church. The covenant is a covenant of grace. God binds Himself to His people in love (John 3:16). God keeps His covenant of love to a thousand generations; even our unfaithfulness cannot nullify it (Romans 3:3).

We are forever engrafted in Christ. Likewise, because the marriage agreement is a covenant, our love for each other in that relationship should also be unconditional and provoke us to extend grace and good works one to the other. The covenant between husband, wife, and God is intended to be the closest, most indissoluble union on earth.

2. Obligation and Responsibility

We have the privilege of knowing God intimately (John 15:13–15; John 17:3) and we share in His unconditional love. But, with privilege comes responsibility! In order for us to receive the full benefit and realize the fulfillment of God's unconditional love, we must embrace God's promise with faith and obedience. This is our obligation according to the covenant we have with God. Receiving Christ involves an end to independent living and the beginning of absolute surrender to Him as Lord. We must place all of our trust in the Lord, remaining faithful and loyal to Him as He is to us.

Likewise, when a man and woman become joined in marriage, mutual love, respect, and faithfulness tie the covenant partners together. Their mutual fidelity is necessary for a successful marriage. The spouses have responsibilities to each other. These are outlined in Scripture. Based on Ephesians 5:33, the book *Love and Respect,* by Dr. Emerson Eggerichs, discusses the obligations that husbands and wives have toward each other. Another excellent book that provides husbands instruction, admonishment, and encouragement in regard to winning the hearts of their wives is *When a Man Loves a Woman, Pursuing Her Heart* by James Ford. For our purposes, this chapter will focus on the obligations of wives.

3. Union and Communion

Finally, our covenant with God features fellowship that grows and extends through time. God Himself spoke to His chosen people, *"I will walk among you and be your God, and you will be my people"* (Leviticus 26:12). God compares His love for us to the marriage relationship to help us understand the tie that binds the partners in the covenant: love and faithfulness (Isaiah 61:10; Jeremiah 3:14; Jeremiah 33:11; Matthew 9:15; Revelation 18). Just as God lavishes us with so great a love that is absolutely binding and irrevocable, it is His intention that a husband and wife have an absolute surrender and deference to each other.

Now that we have established the serious, binding nature of the marriage covenant, will you give your strength to uphold it?

THE POWER OF AFFIRMATION AND CONTENTMENT

Here is a great observation for every woman of God to consider. Proverbs 14:1 says, *"The wise woman builds her house, but with her own hands the foolish one tears hers down."* A woman who realizes the power of affirmation and contentment is a wise woman. Scripture also characterizes her by the honor she gives to her husband: *"Her husband is respected at the city gate, where he takes his seat among the elders of the land."* And, *"Her children arise and call her blessed; her husband also, and he praises her"* (Proverbs 31:23, 28).

I am convinced that the most significant way to honor your husband is with a show of gratitude for who he is and what he does. Gratefulness is best exemplified with a cheerful countenance. A wife who is always unhappy and complaining offers an indictment, not only against her husband, but against God as well. She implies by her sour disposition that neither of them is capable of taking care of her or pleasing her!

Keep in mind that when we as wives love and respect our husbands unconditionally, the demonstration of that love is not predicated on the actions of that man but on the godly character of his wife. If I really love my husband, I love him despite what he does AND I will demonstrate that love! This is a tall order, yet it is nothing new to us as members of the body of Christ, since we are even called to love our enemies (Matthew 5:44; Luke 6:27, 35)! God does not just give us this difficult mandate. He gives us the internal power and resolve to be able to live above our circumstances and to also demonstrate His character.

AN ATTITUDE OF GRATITUDE

Gratitude is letting others know through my words and behavior how they have benefited my life. Etymologically, the central meaning of the word *gratefulness* is "being pleased and making it known." There are three aspects of gratefulness. First, gratitude requires **recognition**. We must be aware of the benefits we have received. Our natural tendency is to be constantly aware of the benefits we extend and take those extended to us for granted. But, when we are grateful, we maintain a constant awareness of daily benefits versus being constantly aware of our disadvantages. It is always sad to see an individual who only becomes acutely alert after experiencing a loss.

Gratitude, once recognized, requires a **response**. After we identify how we have been blessed, our realization requires an appropriate response. There is a very helpful book entitled *The Blessing* by Gary Smalley and John Trent (2004). It gives specific details on how to give unconditional love and honor through the biblical practice of bestowing a blessing.

Finally, gratitude requires **responsibility**. The most significant way to communicate gratitude to our benefactor/husband is through our stewardship and generosity. The way we utilize the gifts given to us demonstrates the degree of our gratefulness.

Embracing Our Femininity

As Christian wives, we should not only be characterized by our home management skills, the way we care for our children, and the like, but we should also be known for how we care for ourselves. In the Song of Solomon, the bride is described as having beautiful skin, lovely hair, and smelling good! Solomon describes Abishag's beauty in three ways:

1. Physically (4:1–5)
2. Emotionally (4:6)
3. Spiritually (4:7)

This is a perfect framework for us. We should not neglect any of these areas. Our care and attention to each category communicates gratitude, because our husbands are just as concerned with these areas as Solomon was. The physical description that Solomon so fervently details for us describes how he appreciates Abishag's loveliness. He indicates that this involves four aspects: being alone with her (4:8); being sexually aroused by her (4:9); his attraction to her desire for him and her lovemaking (4:10); and how her sweet disposition and smell were fascinating to him (4:13–14). His emotional depiction reveals how she affects him, and his spiritual narrative clearly details how much he admires her.

Here are some specific suggestions that can help you in expressing gratitude and affirmation to your husband:

- Make your home a sanctuary and place of rest and refuge (Proverbs 31:11, 20)
- Maintain a good spiritual life (1 Peter 3:1–2, 7)
- Keep yourself beautiful (Song of Solomon). Don't neglect the inner person either! (1 Peter 3:3–5)
- Show an interest in his problems, concerns; offer suggestions, advice, and reproofs when needed in a loving manner (Philippians 2:3–4; Proverbs 31:26; Ephesians 4:25)
- Be his #1 cheerleader, industrious, frugal, diligent, ambitious, and a creative problem solver (Psalm 128:3; Proverbs 31:10–31)
- Frequently express gratitude for his contributions to you personally and your family collectively (1 Corinthians 7:34)

THE PRECEPT: SUBMISSION IN MARRIAGE

A healthy marriage is characterized by love and respect. Ephesians 5:22–28 defines the roles of husband and wife this way:

Wives, submit to your husbands as to the Lord. For the husband is the head of the wife as Christ is the head of the church, his body, of which he is the Savior. Now as the church submits to Christ, so also wives should submit to their husbands in everything. Husbands, love your wives, just as Christ loved the church and gave himself up for her to make her holy, cleansing her by the washing with water through the word, and to present her to himself as a radiant church, without stain or wrinkle or any other blemish, but holy and blameless. In this same way, husbands ought to love their wives as their own bodies. He who loves his wife loves himself.

The discussion of submission is not a topic that is readily embraced by women in general, and it is an especially controversial subject among Black women. Slavery, Jim Crow, segregation, and federal welfare programs that demanded women to be single parents in order to qualify for financial assistance all required Black women to be strong, resilient, brave, and independent in the absence of their fathers, brothers, and husbands.

I have been inspired by the wonderful heritage I have received in women of character and determination, like Harriet Tubman, Mary McLeod Bethune, Phillis Wheatley, and Rosa Parks. They were all stalwart in civil rights, gave voice to those who had none, and even established an institution of higher learning with "$3 and a prayer."

I was raised by a single mother, so I crossed the threshold of married life ill-equipped to live with my husband in a marriage built on biblical principles. Not only was my mom a single parent, but most of the women in my family and their friends were single parents. I admired the women in my family for their strength and fortitude as anchors in our family.

According to a study by Allen-Benton (2004), today's high-functioning young African American woman who has never been married is increasingly apprehensive and insecure about marriage based on six major themes, including:

> perceptions of marriage, expectations for balancing work and family, criteria for a perfect mate, dating experiences, the African American family and spirituality. . . . concern[ed] about the eligibility of the men in the dating pool than the ratio of males to females. They are looking for mates who share their core values of spirituality, goal oriented, family oriented and they are looking for supportive partners. (Allen-Benton 2004)

These concerns point to the decline of marriage and strongly suggest that contemporary African American marriages are far from perfect and definitely do not exemplify the Cliff and Clair Huxtable characters. I approached my marriage thirty-five years ago with similar misgivings.

I was well on my way to establishing a very independent, self-directed lifestyle. I couldn't understand why I had to be subject to my husband when I was the one with a college degree, made more money than he did, owned my own car, had traveled internationally, AND I had known the Lord the longest! I had the upper hand, according to my assessment. Fortunately, my husband was very self-assured and not at all intimidated by my accomplishments or my confidence.

Biblical submission is not contingent on who brings the most experience, education, or expertise to the marriage. Admittedly, biblical marriage roles have not always been taught or modeled. Too often, a pseudosubmission, characterized by oppression and domination, has been presented in place of genuine submission. Authentic submission is not coerced. Instead, a wife willingly defers to her husband's leadership out of obedience to God's Word. Ephesians 5:33 is clear: *"However, each one of you also must love his wife as he loves himself, and the wife must respect her husband"* (emphasis mine). We must obey God in these matters whether our spouses respond or not. We don't practice respect in order to have our love needs met, as important as they are. Our first objective must be to obey and please the Lord.

Even though I did not have an example of biblical marriage in my family, God provided a wonderful example through the lives of my pastor and his wife. When I was a teen, my pastor's wife served as my mentor. She was a strong leader and became my role model. Her life was a wonderful picture of how a godly wife should live. She was a speaker, musician, and prolific writer; a passionate, charismatic visionary who loved her children and lived in harmony with her husband.

A Divine Calling

Despite the fact that I had a godly example, I did not view marriage as a calling from God or my relationship with my husband a divine appointment—at first. Yet I came to realize that marriage is a calling and a ministry, not only to my immediate family, but to those who observe us just as I was encouraged by my pastor and his wife. This realization motivated me to discover what God expected from me as a wife. As I sought the Lord, I discovered that there were things in my heart that were preventing me from trusting Him moment by moment with the charge to submit to my husband. My number one challenge and hesitation? Fear.

Overcoming Fear

For God did not give us a spirit of timidity, but a spirit of power, of love and of self-discipline. (2 Timothy 1:7)

Fear is paralyzing. Fear stymies and short-circuits our ability to trust God and have every confidence in Him to handle things for us! In my case, I was afraid to leave final decisions to my husband early in our marriage because I was afraid. I was afraid because my husband and I were told that our marriage would not last. Honestly, there were observers at our wedding who took real wagers that we would not be married six months from our wedding day!

Talk about prophets of doom. I was afraid because I questioned my own ability to be a good wife. I was afraid that he may be unfaithful at some point. I was afraid to trust my husband's leadership, and my insecurity and apprehension kept me guarded and determined to protect myself. This is not what God has in mind for married women! God wants us to have a full and meaningful life in marriage and apart from it (John 10:10).

The first order of business for me in regard to becoming the wife God intended for me to be was to deal with my hesitation to trust. I came to realize that even if I could not have complete confidence in my husband, I could have total confidence in God! So, I stayed in His Word and received encouragement from 2 Timothy 1:7, and Proverbs 29:25 also spoke very powerfully to me: *"Fear of man will prove to be a snare, but whoever trusts in the Lord is kept safe."* God used these passages to shift my focus from fear of the future and the unknown. He taught me to turn away from a preoccupation with my husband's responsibilities. These were circumstances beyond my control. Rather, I was to center my attention on changing the behavior of the one person who I am responsible for—me!

For that I needed focus on the Lord. I felt secure in God. I began to anticipate love from my husband based on my faith in God and my husband's determination to fulfill God's purposes in his life. I came to terms with negative statements others made about me, especially those I had received as truth. I became very intentional in seeing myself through God's lens. As I began to agree with Psalm 139:14 and express my gratitude to God, I exclaimed, *"I praise you because I am fearfully and wonderfully made; your works are wonderful, I know that full well."*

Trusting God to Honor His Chain of Command

I had to learn how to follow my husband's leadership—whether he was right or wrong! Yes, it is difficult, but God honors obedience to His Word. Of course, this does not mean that a wife should defer if her husband is asking her to commit illegal activity or any act that contradicts God's Word. Rather, this is a realization that husbands are not always going to make decisions we are comfortable with. Scripture further exhorts wives to act as a *helpmeet*. *"The Lord God said, 'It is not good for the man to be alone. I will make a **helper** suitable for him'"* (Genesis 2:18, emphasis mine). The word "helper" denotes collaboration, assistance, advice, partner, and colleague.

Therefore, wives should be available to give prayerful and well-thought-through advice, counsel, and admonishment. Once this valuable input has been volunteered, she must be willing to support the final decision of her husband. In the midst of wrong decisions, respecting his leadership will invite the covering of God for the godly wife! First Peter 3:7 exhorts, *"Husbands, in the same way be considerate as you live with your wives, and treat them with respect as the weaker partner and as heirs with you of the gracious gift of life, so that nothing will hinder your prayers."*

Blessing That Comes from Obedience

When my second child was two years old, I started work on a master's degree in education. This represented a major challenge. My husband had never witnessed a woman with children working away from home. On the other hand, mothers in my family were always working mothers. I was admonished with "counsel for survival" to "always be able to take care of you, girl," and have a personal "stash."

Even though I felt very strongly about working, I also believed that if I worked without my husband's support and permission, I would not be happy. I knew that I would be out from under his authority if this were to happen. I sought the counsel of our pastor at the time, and he suggested that I should try to convince my husband to allow me to work. The economy was bad and we needed the additional income.

I didn't feel comfortable with my pastor's counsel and went home to spend time in prayer. I felt strongly impressed to ask God without precisely knowing what Scripture to read. Then the Holy Spirit led me to Colossians 3:18: *"Wives, submit to your husbands, as is fitting in the Lord."* The King James Version states, *"submit yourselves to your own husbands."* There was my answer. My husband had already told me how he felt about me working away from home.

Later, after our children were school-aged and I was working on my PhD, my husband encouraged me with a significant blessing. I was feeling very overwhelmed with work, the children, and my studies. I went to my husband and told him I was going to quit school because it was simply too much for me to handle. He responded that many years before, I had honored him by submitting to his leadership in regard to working and he wanted to be a blessing to me! He told me to quit my job. He worked very hard that year in order for me to complete my work and have my degree conferred. God honors obedience to His Word.

CONCLUSION

My husband has always reminded me of God's favor upon our marriage. His openness to God makes it easy for me to accept his leadership, knowing that God is our foundation and security. Many young Black women are looking for the ideal man; they can vigorously recite a list of their top ten "must-haves." My admonishment to you, young ladies, is give your expectations to the Lord and let Him make that all-important choice for you by sending the man to find you! Stay busy with your normal routine, accountabilities, friends, family, and hobbies and allow that special someone to find you just like Jacob found Rachel. And please remember, there is no perfect man, *"for all have sinned and fall short of the glory of God"* (Romans 3:23).

For those of us who are married, we must acknowledge the power and significance of the covenant we have entered into, exhibit affirmation and contentment in our marriage, and be willing to submit to the leadership of our husbands. We should be known for our godly character, evidenced by the honor we give to our husbands, as the Bible describes the woman who loves God and her husband: *"She is clothed with strength and dignity; she can laugh at the days to come . . . Her children arise and call her blessed; her husband also, and he praises her: 'Many women do noble things, but you surpass them all'"* (Proverbs 31:25, 28–29). We will know that God is pleased when our husbands respond with affirmation: *"How beautiful you are, my darling! . . . There is no flaw in you . . . and the fragrance of your perfume better than any spice"* (from Song of Solomon chapter 4).

Marriage is the most sacred institution on earth because it is divinely ordained by God. After thirty-five years of being married, I am a living witness that this earthly journey can be a heavenly experience!

REFERENCES

Allen-Benton, Linda. 2004. *Understand How Young High Functioning African American Women Perceive Marriage and Their Thoughts about Remaining Single*. Thesis in Human Development, Virginia Polytechnic Institute and State University. http://scholar.lib.vt.edu/theses/available/etd-05202004-134823/unrestricted/contents.pdf.

SUGGESTED READINGS

Blackman, Lorraine. et.al. 2005. *Consequences of marriage for African Americans*: A comprehensive literature review. Alex Roberts Institute for American Values (212). New York, New York.

Cole, Michael. 1993. "The Christian Marriage." Bible Study. http://www.westarkchurchofchrist.org/library/christianmarriage.htm. West Ark Church of the Christ, www.westarkchurchofchrist.org.

Conrad, Celicia. September 22, 2008. "Black women: the unfinished agenda." http://www.prospect.org/cs/author?id=2097 The American Prospect. www.prospect.org/black.

Eggerichs, Emerson. 2004. *Love & Respect: The Love She Most Desires; The Respect He Desperately Needs*. Nashville: Thomas Nelson.

Ford, James. 2004. *When a Man Loves a Woman, Pursuing Her Heart*. Chicago: Moody.

Haltzman, Scott, and Theresa F. DiGeronimo. 2008. *The Secrets of Happily Married Women: How to Get More Out of Your Relationship by Doing Less*. San Francisco: Jossey-Bass.

O'Quinn, Michael and Doretha. 2007. *What It Takes to Make a Marriage Work*. Unpublished.

Raspberry, W. 2005. "Poor Marriages, Poor Health." *Washington Post*. http://lists101.his.com/pipermail/smartmarriages/2005-October/002828.html.

Smalley, A., and John Trent. 2004. *The Blessing*. Revised updated edition. Nashville: Thomas Nelson.

Wetzstein, C. 2005. "Marriage Found to Improve Black Lives." *Washington Times*. http://lists101.his.com/pipermail/smartmarriages/2005-October/002828.html.

Wilcox and Wolfinger. 2005. "Religion & Marriage Among African Americans in Urban America." *The Fragile Families and Child Wellbeing Study.* http://www.acf.hhs.gov/healthymarriage/pdf/wilcox.brookings.6.04_rev.ppt#2 56,1,Religion & Marriage Among African Americans in Urban America.

Chapter Ten

A SINGLE MOTHER'S ASSIGNMENT: RAISING BOYS TO BE GODLY MEN

For you created my inmost being; you knit me together in my mother's womb. I praise you because I am fearfully and wonderfully made; your works are wonderful, I know that full well. My frame was not hidden from you when I was made in the secret place. When I was woven together in the depths of the earth, your eyes saw my unformed body. All the days ordained for me were written in your book before one of them came to be.

PSALM 139:13–16

Victoria Saunders Johnson

To My Unborn Baby,

Sometime in June of 1988, God quietly and tenderly placed you in my womb. I have no idea of the exact time or day. It will be weeks before I know you exist. But you are not alone. The Divine Team surrounds you—singing you love songs, tickling the bottom of your itty-bitty feet, and regulating the temperature in my human holding tank—making sure you are all right.

Even before any stars were hung in the sky or any ocean waves hit a waterless universe—you were birthed in God's mind. Jesus walked through the heavenly warehouse and selected your silky black curls, your almond-shaped eyes, and cream-colored skin. He decided upon your great father, handpicked your aunties, and posted two older sisters—one at your right side and one at your left side. Their mission was to overwhelm you with "ooo's and ahhh's." In the intellectual part of you, God placed insight beyond your years and in your tiny psyche He molded an unusual, sweet male sensitivity.

You were on God's mind and carried in His heart long before my womb carried you. Each chapter of "'Dre's Story" had already been carefully crafted and written down long before your life began. Your decisions, conversations, challenges, and joys come as no surprise to God. Each baby step, each path you choose as an adult—God has already taken a step ahead of you and blazed the trail. I shout along with David, the psalmist: "Such knowledge is too wonderful for me, too lofty for me to attain" (Psalm 139:6). Before the nurse in the labor room wrapped your fresh new body in a warm blanket, you were already wrapped tight in an untouchable blanket of God's love.

I was sick the entire pregnancy with you, constantly walking around with a cup of herbal tea. Almost everything I ate or smelled made me sick to my stomach. In those early months I remember hunkering down in front of our small window air conditioner, praying for your development and for the nausea to stop. The sick-to-my-stomach feeling never ended so the intense prayers for you continued throughout the entire pregnancy. Even back then I believe God was trying to tell me, "this child will need to be bathed in constant prayer."

The hospital hullabaloo after your birth was electrifying. I can still hear the pride and excitement in your father's voice each time he called a relative or friend to announce, "It's a boy!" His face was beaming; meanwhile, your sisters were whooping, hollering, and running wild through their bedroom back home.

After all the excitement died down in the hospital, I finally got a private moment with you. If the hospital staff would have allowed it (and it wasn't in the middle of winter), I would have taken you outside and lifted you high above my head. Like the ritual carried out in the movie called *Roots*, I wanted to dedicate you to the Lord. Instead, as you lay in my arms, my heart lifted you high into the air. I cried as I thanked God for you. What a special Valentine's Day gift that God had given me on February 14, 1989—your birthday!

During my private dedication service that night in my hospital room, I envisioned God's strong hands opening wide. I carefully placed you inside His palms. I sensed the Heavenly Father's presence walking you around my bed; Jesus standing next to the Heavenly Father praying over you and the Holy Spirit hovering close. It was one of those intimately close moments with the Lord that I wanted to last forever.

THE PLIGHT OF THE BLACK MALE

When my male child turned eighteen, his name was entered on the American blackboard labeled "endangered species." At first, I strongly resented the idea of my precious son being categorized like an eagle or a whale. On the other hand, when animals are labeled on the brink of possible extinction, it seems to touch the heartstrings of people. They rally around and do what they can to preserve the vulnerable one. Unfortunately, our society has yet to sound the alarm concerning the valuable lives of Black males as author Raymond Winbush (2002) describes:

> The cultural and social obstacles facing young African American males today are huge and vastly different from those of just five years ago. If the current rate of homicidal violence among Black males existed in white males, a national crisis would be declared, followed by a White House Conference to address the problem . . . Twenty eight percent of Black men will enter state or federal prisons compared to 16 percent of Latino and 4 percent of white males. If this trend continues by year 2013 half of all Black men in America will be in contact with the criminal justice system.

In addition to these bleak statistics, consider the infant mortality rate of Black babies, genocidal abortion in the African American community, the increasing death rate of African American men with AIDS, mediocre health care, and the rising rate of suicide. Lord, have mercy!

African American mothers in Black churches across the country used to gather in the front of the altar dressed in crisp white uniform-like dresses to fold the Communion cloth on first Sundays. Now, in a huge number of churches across the country, mothers are gathering, but it has nothing to do with the Lord's Supper. They stand at the church altar heartbroken. They've exchanged their white linen dresses for mourning T-shirts labeled "Mothers Against Violence" across their chests and on the back, pictures of their dead sons are displayed. One mother shared, "My son was shot in the head and they say he was probably dead before he even hit the floor."

Just recently, an article hit the newspapers about a gun being given to a child by a parent to go settle a conflict he was having with another boy at school. This kind of behavior was unheard of among parents in past years. If you got in trouble at school, you expected trouble and a good spanking waiting for you at home. Today, it's not uncommon to hear stories about a mother who has been summoned to school because her son has caused a problem. Surprisingly, the irate mother upholds his misbehavior by cursing out the teacher and the principal. In one last stroke of disgust, she dares them to ever call her at work again!

Jawanza Kunjufu identifies this plethora of crises and problems affecting our sons as a conspiracy or genocide, an all-out effort to wipe out an extremely powerful race (Kunjufu 1996). One speaker, Michelle Obelton, compares it to the edict that went out over the male children in Israel in the beginning of the book of Exodus. The pharaoh commanded all the Hebrew male children to be killed, threatened by their growing numbers. She concludes that the same edict has been pronounced against African American males today (Michelle Obelton, Wings Ministries).

Sometimes, my inner being aches as I cry, pray, and plead with God: "What can be done to save my son, our sons?" Plenty of answers are being presented as I stretch out in front of the television, flipping channels with remote in hand. Numerous programs and personalities (Oprah, Dr. Phil, and Bill Cosby) hit the airwaves on any given day talking about how to save our sons. The documentaries, sitcoms, talk shows, and movies all deliver their best advice on mothering an at-risk child.

THE PRINCIPLE

In this chapter, I will not be spending a great deal of time analyzing the problem of violence and the lack of well-being or unhealthy patterns of the African American male. There are several books on the market (some I list at the end of the chapter) about these subjects. What I want to do is present a challenge to mothers of our day, especially Black Christian mothers: How do we step forward and step up to the task of turning this deadly tide that is sweeping our communities and threatening the very survival of our sons? Does God Almighty, Creator of mothers, sons, and motherhood have the answers? Have we sought Him for His solutions and taken the time to listen and follow His instructions?

Seeking biblical answers. Something inside of me, I believe it's the Holy Spirit, pushes me to turn the pages of Scripture and listen to the choir of biblical women singing the songs of deliverance to me. At times, when studying women in the Bible, some of the personalities come across as stiff, nunlike figures draped in ancient robes, speaking the King James English. Then, there are times when I open the Bible and a female biblical character catches my attention. She touches my heart. A "sister-girlfriend" who would place in front of me a plate of chicken wings and collard greens. She says, "Come, sit down in my kitchen and let me tell you a thing or two." With tear-filled eyes, she attempts to tell me her story to help me guide others like myself on our journey—a twenty-first-century Mama raising a Black son.

Two such biblical mothers are Rebekah (Genesis 24) and the Shunammite woman (2 Kings 4). I envision them swinging open the gate of the heavenly choir loft and stepping out into my world. The common thread of love for our sons and our love for God erase the huge cultural gap. God has placed the names and stories of women in His Word because He knew we would be desperately searching for answers. Mothers in our time raising sons are asking as they have been down through the years: How do we successfully move our babies from boyhood to manhood?

The most rigid intellectual biblical scholar melts and describes the love story between Rebekah and Isaac as it is outlined in Genesis, chapter 24; it is truly a romantic affair. Abraham sent his trusted servant, probably Eleazer, to find his son Isaac a bride. After a prayerful and God-ordained mission, Eleazer returns with Rebekah. She rode in on a camel with her company of maidservants. Isaac was out in the field praying. When he looked up and met Rebekah's glance—it was love at first sight.

However, this beautiful love story comes to a screeching reality check after Rebekah had been married for almost twenty years. She had produced neither a little Isaac nor a little Rebekah. Then when Isaac prayed, Rebekah miraculously conceived not one but two children. The births of Esau and Jacob were the first recorded account of twins in the Bible. From the very start, even before they made their entrance into the world, the twin boys fought each other in the womb.

Rebekah, the first female in Scripture to inquire of the Lord, asked, *"Why is this happening to me?"* (Genesis 25:22). In other words, she was thinking,

Lord, what's going on in there? What's all this movement and striving about? The
Lord answered her, *"two nations are in your womb, and two peoples from within
you will be separated; one people will be stronger than the other, and the older
will serve the younger"* (Genesis 25:23).

I've gotta fix this. Rebekah regressed from this touching, prayerful moment
with God. God clearly spoke the promise to Rebekah that her younger son
would assume leadership of the family as opposed to her eldest son. God
planned to work it out. Yet, Rebekah did not wait on God to work it all out.
I can hear her saying something like this: "I could not let God fix it in His own
time and His own way. God gave me the promise before my sons were born,
but I felt like I had to see to it being fulfilled. I could not trust God to work
without my help. I helped my younger son, Jacob, trick his father into giving
him the birthright over his older son, Esau. This cost me Jacob. Esau was so
mad that he threatened to kill Jacob and I had to send him away. Then I
turned back to live without my son and the other son's anger and their father's
mistrust of me."

I can identify with Rebekah. The beautiful, holy hospital scene of giving
my infant son over to the Lord changed quickly for me as well. By the time
Andre was toddling around, I was already trying to figure out *how am I going
to fix this?* I distinctly remember the "Red Airplane Christmas."

When I first married, I wanted four boys. I grew up in a family with two
sisters and no brothers. I wanted sons, mainly so that I could finally play with
trucks and race cars. I know, it sounds crazy, but the toys meant for boys always seemed more fun and interesting to me than dolls and tea sets.

So, when I got pregnant a few months after I got married, I thought *surely,
I'm carrying my first son,* only to be greeted nine months later by a beautiful
baby girl. Three years later, I got pregnant again and I said, "Surely now,
Lord—a son!" Then came daughter number two. I gave up. My dream of having a son was slowly becoming just that—a dream.

One of my husband's co-workers had six girls and then had a son. He'd
teased us constantly: "Man, you just might have to have a half-dozen girls before you get that boy!" My husband would look in my direction and, like the
cute little boy on the Pepsi commercial, I'd stare back defiantly—*don't even
think about it!*

As my due date approached and the possibility loomed in the air that my baby might be born on Valentine's Day, I had a sneaking suspicion that God planned to give me a very special gift—my first and only son!

On the night that he was born, my eyes were fixed on the heavenly trio surrounding him: Father, Son, and Holy Spirit, protecting him and blessing him. By the time he turned two or three years old, my spiritual eyeglasses were already cloudy. My vision of him in God's hands had changed. He was now *my* son. The fate of his life was now in *my* hands.

I distinctly remember the Christmas when I realized that I had the "I gotta fix this" mentality. His father and I were completing our Christmas shopping when he spotted this gigantic plastic red airplane in Toys-R-Us. "Let's get this," he said. I argued, "We've already gotten the kids gifts. We don't have any more money for toys. Where are we going to hide it until Christmas? We can't even get it in the car. We always do the same number of gifts for the kids and this is going to be an extra one. You know how the girls count everything. They'll feel bad if Andre gets an extra gift." But, nothing I said mattered. One of the men from the church picked up the red plastic airplane in his van and hid it at his house until Christmas.

It was truly a "father and son" Christmas that year. My older daughter went to her room crying, because, of course, she counted and felt slighted because of the extra gift for her little brother. However, this wasn't just some run-of-the-mill extra Christmas gift; it was a GIGANTIC one. Andre and his dad sat on the floor for hours with that stupid plastic airplane, swirling it around and laughing. It was as if the girls and I weren't even in the room.

This was the first time I remember thinking, *I'm going to have to fix this. We are spending too much money on Christmas. Dad is showing bias to Andre over the girls. The girls are jealous of Andre.* Before I married, I had dreams and visions of what my family should look like, smell like, and act like. Somehow things were not measuring up—I had to fix it. A spirit of discontentment settled in the back room of my heart.

Rebekah and I both started out great—mothers praying over our pregnancies and our children. Turning to God and listening for His answers, insight, and wisdom. What happened? When did the "I've got to fix this" mind-set come in?

My son entered school and the typical African American male edict was pronounced over him: "He's smart but slow. He's moving at a different pace than his classmates. He's learning but he seems to learn differently than his classmates." I started my scrambling and searching—doing all I could to help my son fit in so that he would do well and be successful. Yes, I prayed, but prayer is a two-way street—putting forward my request before God and then listening for His answers. But back then, I know that I didn't hold still long enough to search out God's mind and listen for His answers.

Rebekah also experienced a "Red Airplane Christmas" moment. She overheard Isaac as he instructed their oldest son, Esau, to go out and bring back a meal. During the meal, Isaac was preparing to pray over him and give him the family blessing. This was the time for Rebekah to remember the promise God gave concerning her younger son before his birth. This was an opportunity for a wife to trust God to work in the heart of her husband.

But, oh no! Rebekah was having none of that! Isaac's plan immediately sent Rebekah into action. She knew exactly what steps to take when she resorted to trickery and manipulation. Rebekah knew God wanted Jacob to be the one to inherit the wealth of his father. Jacob was destined to conduct the business and spiritual affairs on behalf of the family—not Esau. *I've got to fix this,* Rebekah concluded. Instead of going *to the Lord,* as she did when she was pregnant and there was a problem, she resorted *to her own devices* for solutions.

Prodigal mothers. I've heard many sermons discussing the prodigal son, but what about prodigal mothers? As I look back over my life, how many times have I done my best to resolve a situation by employing manipulative tactics rather than turning to the Lord? At those times, I convinced myself that their father does not understand. He's being too hard on the children or too soft. He's favoring one over the other.

Instead of spending time in prayer and seeking the Heavenly Father, I'd resort to my own solutions drawn from my foregone conclusions. When I witness my son taking matters into his own hands, not being patient and failing to take time to seek the Lord, do I have to wonder where he learned this kind of behavior? Jacob became a "master schemer," skills he learned from the actions of his mother.

When mothers do what they think is best for their sons and do not listen to the Lord, the consequences can be serious and costly. In Rebekah's case, she had to send Jacob away because Esau threatened to kill him after he found out Jacob stole his birthright. When Jacob returned home twenty years later, his mother was dead.

However, at this point we need to interject two well-used words: *But God*! Jacob was forced to leave home because of the deception of his mother and the hatred of his brother. He set out as a sojourner, searching for his mother's family. During this twenty-year time period away from home, Jacob turned to God. No doubt he missed his mother. Besides, he had to face down many fears as he traveled in unknown territory and worried about his future.

Nevertheless, his anxiety caused him to take the appropriate action: praying and seeking God. One encounter with God during his travels left him with a serious limp, reminding him not to strive or play games with God. Jacob's difficulties, as a young adult, produced maturity in him. The trials that he experienced developed him to become the godly father of twelve sons. Those sons eventually became the twelve tribes of Israel!

When Bill Cosby made his controversial statements back in 2004, challenging African American parenting practices, he came down hard on mothers. Yes, it's true, the poor choices a mother makes do affect the lives of her children. However, that is not the end of the story. The point is well made in the life of Jacob; in spite of Mama's mistakes and poor choices, Jacob developed into a great man of God. He had his own encounter with God and accomplished that which God set out for him to do.

Dear Andre,

I wish that I had been able to do more to shield you from the freight train coming down the track of our marriage at lightning speed. It was about to hit our family. I had no idea by the time you turned nine years old, our perfect family photos would be ripped into a thousand tiny, painful pieces. I can only imagine the hole in your heart when I had to tell you those horrible words: "your dad is not going to live here anymore." I faced the challenge of moving you toward manhood without a father in the home.

I know now that I should have had your dad present when I delivered this devastating news. There should have been lots of hugs and reassurances about the future, but I had never traveled this road before and unlike preparing for motherhood, I did not prepare ahead of time for a family breakup. I made so many mistakes—not only did a major crisis hit our home, causing a proverbial family train wreck that led to years of marital conflict, ending in an ugly divorce. I stayed on the train tracks bleeding, suffering in pain and depression for way too long. It took some time to realize God's presence and willingness to heal our wounds and mend the broken pieces of our fractured family. When I realized He could put us back together—you and your sisters were well into your teen years.

You were only four years old when the onslaught of family breakup bombs began to hit the house. The girls had school to attend each day, but you were home with me. You've always been an extremely sensitive child. You did not say much, but your spirit seemed to absorb my pain.

Remember our first holiday without your father? I called it a disaster, but you still call it one of our best Christmases ever. You said, "We learned a lot." We were on the bus and we watched grocery store after grocery store turn off their lights and close their doors right before our eyes. A freak snowstorm came up and the buses were running an hour or more behind time. It was the holiday, after all, and the stores closed early. We didn't make it. We came home with no holiday groceries. I managed to fix spaghetti and turkey legs for dinner.

Several times, with tears in your eyes, you've attempted to tell me about your "no daddy here for me" pain. My only hope is that somewhere down your lonely, confusing road, you, like Jacob, will have a God encounter. I pray that you will meet God for yourself, that He will comfort you and move you to a place of humility and submission before Him. Whether your dad and I had stayed together enjoying the perfect life or we ended up in divorce court—either way—you need to encounter God for yourself.

I can almost picture God's delight as He watches you. I don't even have to ask Him what He thinks of you. I can only imagine His broad smile as I call out your name before Him. I feel His hand of comfort and reassurance when I worry about you and wonder if you are going to be okay. I hear Him say re-peatedly, "I made him. I'll watch over him. I've got this. He's going to be alright! You go on to sleep. You go on to work. He's My boy and I will see to him. Your worry, anxiety, anger, and doubt will not add another inch to his height. It's wasted energy and time. Believe Me. Believe in Me. Commit to Me the work of My hands."

THE PRACTICAL

Rebekah lays out the principle lessons for raising a son through a crisis. However, as I read the account of the Shunammite woman, she comes along and lays out the practical application. She comprises the prayer list for us twenty-first-century Black mothers and how we need to pray for our sons.

Like Rebekah, the probability of the Shunammite woman conceiving a child seemed like an impossible dream. In fact, when the prophet Elisha told her that she would have a child as a payment for her hospitality and generosity toward him, I can only imagine her response in modern day slang, with one hand raised and the other on her hip, saying, "Don't play with me."

Scholars conclude that her husband was an older man and the chances of her bearing a child were very slim. God granted Elisha's request on her behalf and she had a son the following year. However, several years later the child got sick in the field with his father and died on his mother's lap. The woman went to find Elisha and pleaded for the life of her son. I believe this mother can teach us a thing or two about what and how to pray for our sons. They may not be dead physically, but many are dead to the things of God.

I've heard the Shunammite woman's story preached several times in a powerful way. The emphasis is usually placed on her faith. In spite of the reality of a dead child, she believed God. She believed that her son would live again. As I read this account over and over again, the Holy Spirit keeps tapping me on the shoulder and pointing out more than the measure of faith that this godly woman possessed. As mothers of sons, there are several areas that give us cause to pray, including the following:

Mothers, pray that God will be welcome in our hearts and homes. First of all, the Shunammite woman went further than the average hospitable woman in her community. She not only opened her home for Elisha, the prophet, to come around for a meal or two—she built a place for him to stay. She encouraged him to visit and made it comfortable for the man of God to do so. I ask the questions of Black mothers today—how much do we really want God around? Do we want His presence in our lives? Have we made room for Him in our hearts? Do we want Him to hold the place of headship in our homes, or do we just want God around in times of emergencies and crisis?

One of my favorite books, *My Heart—Christ's Home: A Story for Young & Old* (Munger 2001), speaks of Jesus entering a house and wanting to live in every corner of the house. He desires to clean out places that have a foul odor or are unpleasant in some way. The house can represent our hearts. Have we ourselves invited Jesus in? Is He important to us? Have we opened every hidden drawer and closet for His inspection and cleansing? Do our children know how important Jesus is to us? Is He our daily bread or just part of an activity that we participate in on Sundays?

My son constantly says to me, "All you know is Jesus. You think Jesus is the answer for everything." He says this in a negative way but when he does, I feel like he has given me one of the best compliments I could ever receive as a mother. On the other hand, I want to guard against always preaching to him. I'd rather that he observe me making Jesus the center of my daily life instead of just hearing me say that Jesus is the center of my life.

Sometimes mothers view church activities as a time to get a break. We are so glad when "Sister So and So" from down the street picks the children up and we can have a few moments of peace at home by ourselves. However, there is an underlying problem with this attitude. It suggests that Jesus is just a Sunday morning habit and not a living part of our lives who helps us thrive. Even subtle things such as our cell phone ring tone—what message is being given out? To us, it may be just a catchy song that we like. But also understand, it's a message your child is hearing each and every time he hears your phone ring.

Some of us have been hurt deeply by the church or even by what we perceive as God forgetting about us. When a child gets molested, neglected, or affected by a loved one who dies early in that child's life, scars are set up in our hearts. Furthermore, it's not easy for God to become a Heavenly Father to us if our earthly fathers have not been what they needed to be in our lives. However, this is why it is so necessary to allow Christ into every area of our lives—

even the hurting, damaged, and confusing parts. He has to be the One to re-script our thinking and mend our hearts to the point where we are comfortable with Jesus residing on the inside of us. Christ must have a significant presence in our lives, and not just be a convenient pain pill when we are in pain.

Purging Anger and Bitterness

This kind of strategic spiritual operation takes time and may require some help from a more mature Christian sister or a counselor. If we are going to stop the wave of anger and violence in our community that is being played out in the lives of our sons, we must be prepared to act decisively, using every necessary means. Just as Rebekah's son inherited her tendency toward manipulation and it manifested itself in Jacob's life, we need to examine what's in our hearts that may be transferred to our children. After you do some serious soul searching, will you find: Anger? Unforgiveness? Bitterness?

I'm very aware that some of the anger and bitterness that fills the heart of my son in regard to his father has been transferred from me to him. I feel an obligation to pray through this so that I can be free, but also so that my son can witness how to effectively work through a situation when someone has wronged you. It's been a long, difficult process but I've opened myself up to Jesus to do whatever He needs to do in me so that the curses of one generation do not transcend to another.

Mothers, pray that our sons will know how important they are to us. I remember the time before my son went to kindergarten. The girls would be gone to school and Andre knew this was *our time*. He looked forward to that and I tried my best to make it special. Even if I had plenty to do with cooking, cleaning, or writing assignments, I made sure he was in the room with me. Andre always had his own task to help me with, and I would talk with him and ask for his opinion and suggestions about the task at hand.

Even after I started working, it was very important for me to spend time with each child alone at night. They looked forward to me individually reading them a story. After the story I would wait for them to fall asleep. I was often dog-tired and irritated by having other things to do, but I asked God to make the time I spent with each child not just one more thing on my list but a time of rest and refreshment for both of us. God never disappointed; I was always pleasantly surprised to come out of their rooms feeling more uplifted than when I went in.

Also, when my children were small, we lived "television-free" for several years. I can still hear the comments from others: *"That's crazy. How are you going to find out what's going on in the world? Your children are going to be too sheltered."* But, instead of vegetating in front of the television set, we read books, went to the YMCA for activities, visited people, and worked on various projects. Mothers, believe it or not, children do not want to be entertained. What they really want is you! You can do the simplest thing with a child, as long as they know they have your undivided attention.

Mothers, pray that our sons will know their value and importance before God. This area, in particular, is very sensitive to me. I wanted my son to know that as a Black child, he should value his self-worth. What better way could he understand than to have someone take a deep interest in him and show him that he is important from God's perspective. He needed a male presence to teach him who he is in God's sight.

After I became a single parent, there was a time when I desperately needed Andre to be exposed to more Christian families who were exhibiting wholeness under the headship of a strong Black man. But there was a deficit of available Christian brothers who could model the qualities of male leadership for him. I attended several churches and inquired of several Christian men and always came back with no help for my son.

I wanted the same kind of support for my girls. But as they grew older, I was able to take them with me to women's retreats and women's Bible studies. It was okay to drag Andre along when he was little. But, as he got older, I searched high and low for men's retreats and camps that would help him move toward Christian manhood. Nothing. However, I found quite a few activities within the Muslim community.

Although there were several non-Christian men available to help my son academically, overall, I've been very disappointed with the availability of Black Christian males who were willing to serve as positive role models. Most seemed too busy with church, work, and other activities that filled their lives to really take time out and help foster another young male.

Furthermore, I wanted my son to read about and see positive images of children who looked like him. For the girls it was always easier for me to find

Christian books about girls their age and the challenges they faced. However, it wasn't as easy to find reading material for Andre. I was always searching and asking teachers and other mothers about books for young Black boys. When we visited the library, the girls would have armfuls of books with children on the cover who looked like them and had shared their experiences. Andre and I would go down aisle after aisle looking for similar books—there were hardly any with positive, affirming images of Black boys.

The messages came early and they came loud and clear: "This is a White male dominated world. You do not belong. You are not an important part of it." I hear and understand that message a lot clearer now and I wish back then I'd had the wisdom to counter some of those negative messages directed to my son. I could have helped him cope with it by saying to him such things as: "The world does not always recognize you as important, but you are very important to God. Everyone doesn't have the ability to write books that can tell little boys how much you mean to God. And, when women have a desire to write, they naturally have a tendency to write to little girls. Black Christian men are busy with so many things, such as raising their families and working to support them. It's hard for them to turn their attention to writing children's books that will encourage young boys.

"Andre, maybe this is a trend you can turn around. You are a good writer; you have talent in this area. You can be sure that there are more books for little boys like you when you get older."

Mothers, pray that God will be a Father to the fatherless. One man finally explained to me that his wife would be intimidated by me. He said that "no brother's wife is going to let him come over to your house and deal with your son. She would think that you are trying to get next to her man." This was very disheartening to me because I have really needed help with my son over the years. Once his dad and I separated, it left a huge void in his life for constant male companionship.

There was another problem that wasn't evident in raising the girls, but I ran into it consistently with my son. I had a lack of understanding in regard to his passage from boyhood to manhood. As a woman, the experiences of my daughters were very familiar to me. I had similar emotional and physical feelings in junior high and high school so I could clearly guide their actions, understand their thoughts and conversations.

However, I really had no clue regarding the feelings of a son and the process of growing up—absolutely no clue. I did not have brothers, so I never had the opportunity to observe or even vicariously experience the transition stages of becoming a man. I knew a lot about grown men, but I had no idea of all the things they went through and felt to get there. Once again, as my son approached these years, I found myself scrambling, cajoling, pleading, and begging his father and other men to help.

I can say in extreme times of crisis my pastor and a few other pastors I know would shoot me a quick e-mail if I asked for their advice and suggestions. They have never failed to advise and to pray. When I call on my spiritual moms in regard to my girls, not only are these ladies there in spirit, but they are also present physically to talk on the phone, exhort, encourage, reprove, hug, and pray for my children. I've watched my girls blossom spiritually as a result of this kind of nurturing. Unfortunately, I've observed just the opposite with my son. Men seem to keep their distance. As a result, I've watched my son wither, feeling left out, rejected, and lost.

To complicate issues, the bond between my ex-husband and my son is extremely tight. I believe my son thinks, *If I bond with another man, Dad may not like it. I may never see him, so I'm going to keep this space open only for my dad.* In one of his honest moments, Andre will admit to the truth of this assessment. One family friend described it as a bondage situation. Andre is not willing to let go of his Dad in a healthy way so he can bond with God and other brothers in the body of Christ.

I've spoken to Andre numerous times about loving his father, but also making room for other relationships that can help him learn about godly manhood. I've encouraged him to allow God to come in and be an ever-present Father to him. Assuredly, God is the only Father who will never leave, forsake, or disappoint him. No earthly father can make this promise!

When our family went through the breakup of my marriage, my girls readily embraced God as their Father. They have nurtured and treasured their relationship with God, and in some ways I see the destruction of divorce as being the catalyst of their true salvation. In a very powerful way, they relate to God and help others who have been through similarly painful experiences. Conversely, Andre has never seen God as his Father first, and his earthly father second. There is a little boy inside him who seems to constantly cry out, *I want my daddy!*

Once again, my tendency is to run frantically around and find a way to fix the problem. Oh, what freedom came the day I reckoned that I can't. I finally reached the conclusion that God is the only One who can fix this situation. I surrendered by praying, "Lord, I totally turn it over to You."

Mothers, pray in utter humility. There is praying and then there is p-r-a-y-i-n-g! When the Shunammite woman got off her donkey to meet Elisha, she talked to him about her son who had died in her lap. However, she did not stand eyeball to eyeball with the prophet, challenging him to discuss the problem. There was no stereotypical Black woman stance. Her left hand was not firmly placed on her hip with the first finger of her right hand wagging in the prophet's face.

That was not the case. This prominent and rich woman, no doubt wearing the finest fabric and robes in Israel, hit the ground. She didn't seem to care that her face was positioned a few inches from where her donkey may have defecated. She wrapped herself around the dirty sandals of Elisha and pleaded for the life of her son. This is an example of serious praying out of utter desperation and humility. It got Elisha's attention and concern. Her conduct caused him to travel back to her home about five to six hours away. He had to go out of his way to attend to one child.

This is a beautiful and symbolic picture of what God is like. He is no respecter of persons. The things God did back in biblical days for His children, He is still willing to do today. But, are we willing to take the stance of the Shunammite woman? Are we willing to humble ourselves and give Him total access to every nook and cranny of our hearts? We have the ability to establish His firm presence in our homes. To bring about that change, are we willing to humble ourselves in serious prevailing prayer?

Mothers, pray that our sons will follow us in submission to those in authority. The Shunammite woman's story does not end in the book of 2 Kings, chapter 4. When Elisha informed this woman that a famine was coming, he advised her to move. She obeyed. Let me repeat that—she obeyed. It put her in a place of blessings because the famine lasted for seven years. She picked up and left her beautiful home and the security of her family and friends to do what Elisha told her. What a profound picture of submission and obedience.

I have spoken to several people, especially women, who view submission as a curse word. Some believe it only applies in marriage and if we are not married, we don't have to be in submission to anyone. However, the Bible is clear. We are to submit to governing authorities, church officials, and bosses. In fact, Scripture tells us that *"everyone must submit himself to the governing authorities, for there is no authority except that which God has established. The authorities that exist have been established by God. Consequently, he who rebels against the authority is rebelling against what God has instituted, and those who do so will bring judgment on themselves"* (Romans 13:1–2).

You can rest assured, there is no authority in place other than those put there by God! If we model rebellion against husbands, bosses, police officers, or pastors—guess who else is going to rebel and have negative attitudes toward those in authority!

In 2 Kings, chapter 8, we see the fruit of the Shunammite woman's submission paying off. She returned home and had to go to the king because someone had taken over her land. She walked in as Gehazi the servant is telling the king the story of how Elisha raised her son from the dead. The king showed compassion and restored her property, as well as the profits that were made on the land while she was away. Her son was with her, watching the hand of the Lord work this situation out in their lives. The favor of God was with her because of her obedience. Had she disobeyed Elisha and insisted on staying put, the story would have had quite a different ending.

Dear Andre,

You have been by my side for several years now. You've watched me, listened to me. You know me better than family or friends. You've seen me at my worst and best. I want you to remember most of all my love for you and the Lord. One or the other cannot be compromised. But, one has to come before the other. My love and obedience to the Lord must always come first.

You've forced me to line up with other mothers praying for their sons to come back to the Lord and walk in their God-given calling. Right now the world and all its bells and whistles are more fascinating to you than the quiet voice of your Heavenly Father calling you, encouraging you to come back to Him.

I'm paying close attention to the father as he dealt with his prodigal son. I'm following in his footsteps, letting you pack up and go the way you insist on going, even though I know it's not the right way and it will end in distraction for you. I imagine the father looking down that road constantly, praying and hoping that you will come home. I also anticipate the day of celebration when you finally understand there is no food and festivity that compares with what God lays out for His children. Everything else is counterfeit and ends up tasting like pig slop in the end. I wait patiently for that day of celebration. I know it's coming!

In the meantime, God is working on me through you. He is instilling unconditional love, forgiveness, and patience inside my heart. By the time you decide to walk with the Lord, we will both be prepared to be part of a mighty army—mother and son—walking together with all the saints, praising God and giving Him all the glory.

REFERENCES

Bureau of Justice statistics on prisoners in 2006, Bul84letin December 2007. http://www.ojp.usdoj.gov/bjs/pub/pdf/p06.pdf.

Kunjufu, J. 1995. *Countering the Conspiracy to Destroy Black Boys*. Vol. IV. Chicago: African American Images Press.

Munger, Robert Boyd. 2001. *My Heart—Christ's Home: A Story for Young & Old*. Downers Grove, Illinois: InterVarsity Press.

Winbush, R. 2002. *The Warrior Method: A Parent's Guide to Raising Healthy Black Boys*. New York: Harper Collins.

SUGGESTED READINGS

Evans, T. 2000. *Tony Evans Speaks Out on Single Parenting*. Chicago: Moody Publishers.

Hrabowski, F. A., K. I. Maton, and G. L. Greif. 1998. *Beating the Odds: Raising Academically Successful African American Males.* Later printing edition. New York: Oxford University Press.

Lawson, Bush V. 1999. *Can Black Mothers Raise Our Sons?* Chicago: African American Images Press.

Williams, K. 2006. *Single Mama Dos and Don'ts.* SingleMamahood Publishing.

Chapter Eleven

A SINGLE MOTHER'S ASSIGNMENT: RAISING GODLY DAUGHTERS

Amanda Johnson

What am I supposed to do now?

This was not the way I planned it. This is nothing like those families that I've watched on TV. I was a preschooler watching Wally and the Beaver. Later, when I was old enough to prepare my own Nestle's Quik, I spent countless hours drinking chocolate milk and watching *Happy Days.*

Not being one to interfere with tradition, my children grew up with the first family of television for their generation: the Huxtables. So, what's goin' on? Doesn't art imitate life? How can I possibly be moving to a new city alone with five daughters? This is not the Cinderella/Snow White/Sleeping Beauty/romanticized/"happily ever after" story that my mom read to me at bedtime.

FAMINE IN THE FAMILY

The disillusionment of my fractured fairy tale was only the beginning. It didn't take long for me to realize that my girls and I were in the middle of an emotional and economic crisis. I was longing for the comfort, support, and companionship of a failed marriage. The girls were feeling the deprivation of being without their dad. The hour of 6:00 p.m. couldn't have been more arid and barren in the Sahara than it was in our new family unit. Those little girl squeals that I could set my kitchen clock to were gone. The frivolity and glee of five girls vying all at once for his attention and talking nonstop to bring Daddy up to speed concerning the happenings of the day had been replaced with stark silence.

Tragically, "home" was the basement floor of a friend's home for three months. Then "home" became a hotel room for three more months—a place full of people who were one day away from the sidewalk. The new social and financial dynamic of our family was the equivalent of a famine.

If you are a single mom, perhaps you are in the throes of a social and/or economic famine. Admittedly, it isn't easy raising children as a single parent. Women who find themselves in this position work hard to financially support their children and themselves; however, poverty too often becomes a reality. The need to produce sufficient income can pose a major test as the stresses of everyday life multiply.

Single mothers face serious challenges in providing decent housing in safe neighborhoods where a quality education is available for their children. In addition, maintaining affordable health care is a necessity that many parents must forgo as the high cost of health insurance makes coverage not an option. Perhaps most importantly, a single mom must tend to the safety of her children by finding sufficient day care and protection while she works.

With all of these issues under consideration, single mothers often experience a cycle of hopelessness and despair, which is detrimental to both themselves and their children. Research suggests that the children of single mothers use mental health services at two to four times the rate of children in two-parent families (Garfinkel & McLanahan 1986), and single mothers experience significantly higher rates of clinical depression, anxiety, and feelings of isolation than do married mothers.

But, the good news is that you have a source of help in the Holy Spirit who covers you with provision and protection. As you do your best to be the mother He created you to be and give the rest to God, you will always come out on top—He will never disappoint you.

Lack of Prosperity in Zarephath: The Dire Consequences of Poverty

The presence of prosperity in one's life is the capability of an individual to acquire food, clothing, shelter, and other consumables that afford a mother and her children the opportunity to have a comfortable existence. Because these necessities are in place, prosperity helps create "space" in the heart, mind, life, and family so that individuals can grow emotionally, spiritually, and socially. When a family prospers, they are relieved of the burden and anxiety that come from a lack of the daily necessities required for utter survival. Therefore, living in prosperity provides an atmosphere that advances and promotes productivity.

The truth is, living with daily deficits can be exhausting, stealing aspirations and the energy to even fight for life. Ask any single mother who is fresh out of options. There was even one in the Bible who had just about reached her limit as she dealt with the reality of poverty. But God had a different ending to her plight; He used the prophet Elijah to intervene in her life:

> *Then the word of the Lord came to him: "Go at once to Zarephath of Sidon and stay there. I have commanded a widow in that place to supply you with food." So he went to Zarephath. When he came to the town gate, a widow was there gathering sticks. He called to her and asked, "Would you bring me a little water in a jar so I may have a drink?" As she was going to get it, he called, "And bring me, please, a piece of bread." "As surely as the Lord your God lives," she replied, "I don't have any bread—only a handful of flour in a jar and a little oil in a jug. I am gathering a few sticks to take home and make a meal for myself and my son, that we may eat it—and die."* (1 Kings 17:8–12)

Wow. Now that's tight. Talk about poverty. You may be thinking right about now, *but, why should I trust God? What's the use? My situation is about as bad as hers. But, God is not about to send a prophet to help me. It's so bad and I don't see how things can ever get any better for me.* But, read on because the story gets better:

> *Elijah said to her, "Don't be afraid. Go home and do as you have said. But first make a small cake of bread for me from what you have and bring it to me, and then make something for yourself and your son. For this is what the Lord, the God of Israel, says: 'The jar of flour will not be used up and the jug of oil will not run dry until the day the Lord gives rain on the land.'"* (1 Kings 17:13–14)

Perhaps your life is full of unmet needs, expectations, and limited opportunities. If that's the case, I empathize. I have been in a place of despair; like the widow in Zarephath, I had nowhere to turn. I was totally bankrupt of spirit. Let me encourage you. Look up! When things appear to be the most dismal and bleak; when you are down to your last dime with a gallon of gas— try hope. That is when God will be compelled to move on your behalf. He may not send a prophet, but rest assured, God knows how to get us the help that we need. This mother's story continues. Notice the key that brought about the solution to her problem:

> *She went away and did as Elijah had told her. So there was food every day for Elijah and for the woman and her family. For the jar of flour was not used up and the jug of oil did not run dry, in keeping with the word of the Lord spoken by Elijah.* (1 Kings 17:15–16)

In times of famine, the best choice we can make is to run to God and obey Him! We should do what God says. Especially when things look dismal, we can rely on God to send help. When God sees us at rock bottom, He will intervene on our behalf. Just like He spoke through Elijah and pointed the woman in the right direction, God will provide the guidance that you need. Although it was a test of her obedience, she passed. It was ultimately an act of obedience that revealed her faith in God and gave her the victory.

Godly Femininity in the Midst of Famine

The Bible teaches us that wisdom is more precious than jewels. And Scripture helps us choose between the two: *"How much better to get wisdom than gold, to choose understanding rather than silver!"* (Proverbs 16:16). Furthermore, when you apply wisdom and understanding from the Word of God, you will learn how to walk out that knowledge in your daily life.

Here is a word of wisdom for you when you are in the midst of famine: Don't speak death. Speak life! Scripture holds a revealing truth that brings immeasurable benefit to a woman of faith: *"The tongue has the power of life and death, and those who love it will eat its fruit"* (Proverbs 18:21). Our speech is an indicator of our faith. The wise woman will carefully watch what she says about her situation. It can mean the difference between failure and victory. The expectations we have for our children are powerful and they tend to live up to them. When we speak faith, it releases God's power to do good for us.

Let me remind you, when you find yourself in a famine, make the decision to obey God. The story of the widow of Zarephath can teach us many things. Here are some significant strategies we can take away from her response to God's direction for her life.

1. Make serving God a priority. The woman stopped what she was doing and put God first when she heard God's direction through His prophet (1 Kings 17:13).

2. We must obey God to put us on the right path to receive God's blessings. The woman "did as Elijah had told her" by following his instructions and returned home (v. 15).

3. Remember that placing our faith and trust in God in the midst of famine produces abundance (vv. 15–16).

4. Believe that when our dreams die in a famine, God can renew and resurrect them (vv. 17–24).

Now that we have established steps that can empower us to survive the deficits of single parenting, let's look at the following reasons for taking our direction from God by approaching parenting from a godly perspective. We will cover the following:

- why parenting should be a priority
- what is godly parenting?
- how to apply tactics that can produce godly living in the lives of our daughters

God would have us make this approach to parenting a daily focus. As we increase in understanding of how to apply these ideas to our lives, it will not only give our daughters the tools they need to grow as Christians, but it will help them through the emotional and/or financial lean times that are typically a part of life.

RIGHT BEGINNINGS:
WHY PARENTING SHOULD BE A PRIORITY

Why Should We Work Hard at Raising Virtuous Daughters?

It Is Part of My Life Purpose

When I decided that I wanted Christ to be in control of my life, one of the first questions I had was in regard to my life purpose. Before I even had children, I prayed, "God, how can I best serve You?" The wonderful thing about having children is once they are born, that question is automatically answered! I was given my assignment by God. He makes it clear that raising children should be our top priority once He appoints us to be parents. Scripture issues a very specific and well-defined mandate to parents in Deuteronomy 6:5–9:

> *Love the Lord your God with all your heart and with all your soul and with all your strength. These commandments that I give you today are to be upon your hearts. Impress them on your children. Talk about them when you sit at home and when you walk along the road, when you lie down and when you get up. Tie them as symbols on your hands and bind them on your foreheads. Write them on the doorframes of your houses and on your gates.*

Teaching our children how to obey, love, worship, and revere God is clearly a priority to Him. We are to be dedicated to teaching and training our children, because of our love and devotion to God (v. 5). In order to accomplish this, we MUST know God's Word and have large portions of it committed to memory (v. 6). As mothers, we are in the best position to make lasting impressions about how much we love, value, and respect God and His Word.

We must whet our children's appetites for the things of God and develop a sensitivity to Him. This is most significantly shown by having a heart for and loving people (v. 7a). In order for this type of reverence to be transferred from mother to daughter, it must be modeled as a lifestyle in every aspect of our daily lives (v. 7b). We must make indelible, lasting impressions on the minds and hearts of our girls concerning the things of God and how to live for Him (vv. 8–9).

Finally, one of the most significant reasons we are going to invest the resources of time, talent, and treasure in our quest to raise virtuous, godly women is to establish a legacy of righteousness. Raising godly children will impact future generations within our families that can significantly affect the moral and ethical fabric of neighborhoods, communities, cities, countries, and ultimately the entire world. Do you have visions of making a national or even a global impact? Do you want to help reach the world for Christ? Then make the sacrifices that are required to raise virtuous daughters who will have the tools necessary to live a meaningful Christian life. You may ask, what is required? I say, be prepared to put your personal pursuits on hold during the child-rearing years!

I contend that the most significant opportunity for biblical discipleship exists within the walls of our homes. The apostle Paul encourages believers in Christ to continue the process of discipleship: *"And the things you have heard me say in the presence of many witnesses entrust to reliable men [and women] who will also be qualified to teach others"* (2 Timothy 2:2). We please God by preparing our daughters to participate in His kingdom-building work. The Bible states in the book of Acts 2:47 that God adds to the church daily.

Furthermore, God encourages His people to "be fruitful and multiply," (Genesis 1:28; 9:1 KJV). So, if you want to make a lasting impact on the world for Christ, RAISE GODLY SONS AND DAUGHTERS. God adds to the church, but He does so by multiplying families! On a daily basis we are able to "live out" the tenets of our faith in front of those God has given us to disciple. This is the most effective way to live out our purpose in life: by teaching our daughters how to live godly, as we "sit at home, walk along the road, lie down, and get up."

The Law Demands It

Quite simply, the law requires that parents are responsible for the behavior of their children. We must teach our children that just as God has laws to uphold, there are civil laws that we must also follow. In Michigan, for example, the statute in the Michigan Compiled Laws states:

600.2913 Minor maliciously or willfully destroying property or causing bodily harm or injury to person; recovery of damages from parents.

Sec. 2913 also states:

A municipal corporation, county, township, village, school district, department of the state, person, partnership, corporation, association, or an incorporated or unincorporated religious organization may recover damages in an amount not to exceed $2,500.00 in a civil action in a court of competent jurisdiction against the parents or parent of an unemancipated minor, living with his or her parents or parent, who has maliciously or willfully destroyed real, personal, or mixed property which belongs to the municipal corporation, county, township, village, school district, department of the state, person, partnership, corporation, association, or religious organization incorporated or unincorporated or who has maliciously or willfully caused bodily harm or injury to a person.

The Bible recognizes that obeying government is a necessity (Romans 13:1–2). I taught my daughters early that there are consequences for our actions. They understand that good behavior brings good consequences; likewise, if one misbehaves, she can expect bad things to happen. To be under His blessings, God expects us to live on the good side of the law.

The Immediate and Future Health of Society-at-Large Requires It

The current state of affairs in America, in general, and the Black community in particular, desperately needs an aggressive and immediate return to a more traditional approach to parenting. By traditional, in this context I mean, at minimum, to be proactive, purposeful, and present! Consider the current state of affairs for Black children, as reported by "The State of America's Children 2008 Report" on the Children's Defense Fund website. Each day in America among Black children:

- **3 children** or teens are killed by firearms.
- **5 children** or teens die from accidents.
- **24 babies** die before their first birthdays.
- **103 children** are arrested for violent crimes.
- **118 children** are arrested for drug crimes.
- **224 babies** are born at low birth weight.
- **292 babies** are born to teen mothers.
- **312 babies** are born without health insurance.
- **439 high school students** drop out.*
- **556 children** are confirmed as abused or neglected.
- **581 public school students** are corporally punished.*
- **755 babies** are born into poverty.
- **1,345 children** are arrested.
- **6,792 public school students** are suspended.*

* *Based on calculations per school day (180 days of seven hours each)*

Need I say more? Our communities are in a state of emergency. Somebody had better do something! And that somebody is us! As Christian parents, moms and dads can delegate our authority to the church and schools, but based on the mandate in Deuteronomy 6:5–9, I am convinced that God is going to hold parents accountable, in the final analysis, for the amount of nurturing we give our children or the lack thereof.

With all of these aspects of parenting to consider, we should agree that single parenting has its own unique challenges. I have presented the reasons why parenting virtuous daughters should be our top priority. Now, let's talk about how we're going to do it.

FIRST THINGS FIRST: WHAT IS GODLY PARENTING?

We Must Be Right with God

We cannot impart what we do not possess. All of the daily disciplines I am going to encourage you to teach your daughters must be a well-established part of your personal routine.

First and foremost, we must keep short accounts with the Lord, confessing any sin as God convicts us of it. Our hearts must be pliable and we must be willing to receive Instruction from God. The Word of God tells us to prepare ourselves: *"Break up your unplowed ground and do not sow among thorns. Circumcise yourselves to the Lord, circumcise your hearts, you men of Judah and people of Jerusalem"* (from Jeremiah 4:3–4).

The phrase "unplowed ground" (NIV) or "fallow ground" (KJV) comes from the Hebrew noun *nir,* which means "untilled land." This land could be productive, but it needs to be broken up, plowed, and prepared for planting. The point is, fallow ground will not yield crops! Nothing can grow on it. It's hard. Seeds cannot penetrate, germinate, or grow to maturity in it. The prophet Jeremiah is cautioning believers to prepare the ground of our hearts before we attempt to plant righteousness. Otherwise, attempting to sow seeds of righteousness among thorns without first preparing the soil of our hearts is an exercise in futility. This means we have to set some things right in our interactions with others. For example, carefully consider the following:

We Must Be Right with the Other Parent

I have acknowledged the financial and emotional pressures of single parenting, but perhaps the most significant challenge of all is managing the pain,
solitude, and vulnerability of being a single mother. Regardless of the route we
took to being a single mom—whether it was through a divorce, an unmarried
pregnancy, or perhaps even death—forgiveness is one thing that most of us
must deal with. And many times we have to deal with it on an ongoing basis.
The primary cause of a heart that needs to be healed is bitterness that is fueled
by a lack of forgiveness. It is imperative that we let go of the pain that a spouse
may have caused us and the only way to do it is to forgive him. Scripture cau-
tions us, *"See to it that no one misses the grace of God and that no bitter root
grows up to cause trouble and defile many"* (Hebrews 12:15).

What is growing in your heart? Unforgiveness? Hatred? Bitterness? If your
answer is any of these, know that, ultimately, harboring harsh feelings hinders
our spiritual growth, rendering us ineffective and useless. If we are shackled by
bitterness and anger, then Satan has us where he wants us—handcuffed to
restlessness and void of God's peace. In other words, our efforts to please God
are derailed. If the Enemy can just get us caught up in a conflict or two that
drains our spiritual energy, then he can beat us down.

In regard to raising godly daughters, the Enemy can stall our efforts, which
is his objective. Since he hates Christianity, he does not want to see it perpet-
uated in the earth. Consequently, he hates children who are being trained to
live godly lives. If you've ever been anxious or angry, then you know how much
these emotions totally absorb your strength. It makes you too tired to pray regarding the real battles because of our preoccupation with the perceived ones!

Overcoming Bitterness

For a single mother, forgiveness is the key that unlocks blessings for you and
your children. In fact, the only solution to overcoming anger with offenders is
to forgive them. Does forgiveness mean that the perpetrator got away with the
wrong? Does it mean that we will passively allow further offenses? Perhaps it
seems unfair that your offender has not and will not pay adequate restitution
for their offense. In her book *Hurt People Hurt People: Hope and Healing for
Yourself and Your Relationships,* Sandra D. Wilson addresses this very typical
concern:

Surely a wound-matching level of repentance would likely make forgiving easier. But would that actually pay for deep wounds caused by repeated betrayals of trust? What could our hurters possibly do today to make up for what they did yesterday? In effect, they owe us debts they can never repay. Our hurters stand before us with empty hands and pockets, utterly unable to pay for the past. And we stand facing the choices that will shape our futures. We can keep trying to collect debts rightfully owed us by exacting verbal and nonverbal tolls, but that means constantly replaying the painful past to keep our hurters' deficits fresh on our mental balance sheets. Or we can cancel their debts and forgive. (1993)

Undoubtedly, our unforgiveness hurts us more than it does our offenders. Bitterness, resentment, and wrath are actually forms of attachment. We unwittingly "bind" ourselves to our offenders as two oxen would be yoked together to plow! To remain in that yoke is bondage of the worst sort. In the article "The Gift of Forgiveness: Giving Up the Emotional Toxins," consider what Dr. Arnold Fox, a noted physician, has discovered about refusal to forgive:

Forgiveness allows your body to turn down the manufacture of those chemicals which are tearing you apart, body and soul. Doctors can give you all sorts of medicines for your headaches, your heart, your stomach pains, your spastic colon, your anxiety, and other problems, but the medicines will not get to the root of the problem: Unforgiveness. The cure for that lies in forgiving. When you savor your hatred, you don't hurt them, you hurt yourself. (1989, 18)

Expressing Bold Love

So, you might ask, do our offenders get away with wrong to commit further offenses? Drs. Dan Allender and Tremper Longman III (1992) answer that question with a resounding "No!" In the book *Bold Love,* they address this question:

Forgiving love is the inconceivable, unexplainable pursuit of the offender by the offended for the sake of restored relationship with God, self, and others. . . . To forgive another is always an ongoing, deepening, quickening process, rather than a once-and-for-all event.

The offended forgives (cancels) the debt by not bringing immediate judgment and termination of the relationship, as might be reasonable and expected, given the offense. Instead, mercy is offered in order to invite the offender back into the relationship. The cost for the offended is in withholding judgment and instead offering the possibility of a restored relationship. The cost for the offender is repentance. Biblical forgiveness is never unconditional and one-sided. It is not letting others go off scot-free, "forgiven," and enabled to do harm again without any consequence. Instead, forgiveness is an invitation to reconciliation. (1992)

My prayer is that you purpose in your heart to allow our loving Father to break up any resentment and bitterness you are nursing toward the other parent. The process of healing the residue of hurt feelings will begin. There is no price to be put on the blessing of being in compliance with God's command to: *"Sow for yourselves righteousness, reap the fruit of unfailing love, and break up your unplowed ground; for it is time to seek the Lord, until he comes and showers righteousness on you"* (Hosea 10:12).

Our Personal Conduct Must Be Righteous

It is always a good thing to pray God's Word back to Him. God loves it when we sincerely want to be righteous and say to Him: *"May the words of my mouth and the meditation of my heart be pleasing in your sight, O Lord, my Rock and my Redeemer"* (Psalm 19:14). This is a personal acknowledgment to God and He will respond by giving us the desires of our heart.

One of the big challenges for many of us will be in the area of taming our tongues. We have to get things resolved with the other parent. We must break up any fallow ground. We cannot harbor bitterness and allow it to come out in negative, disparaging comments about the child's father. He may just be "yo' baby daddy" to you, but to that little girl, I can almost guarantee that he is her hero, her knight in shining armor, her "all that," and more!

We can demand obedience from our daughters, but we must earn their respect. And, disrespectful behavior breeds disrespect! Scripture says that, as much as possible, we should *"turn from evil and do good; seek peace and pursue it"* (Psalm 34:14) and *"make every effort to live in **peace with all men** and to be* *holy"* (Hebrews 12:14, emphasis mine).

The truth is that children love both of their parents, and unless your child's father poses some imminent danger to you or her, you should work hard to have a civil, if not friendly, relationship with him. You will receive great benefits from your actions: Your child will thank you for it, you will contribute to her positive emotional development, and God will be pleased with how you handle the responsibility you have toward your children.

Follow Me as I Follow Christ!

There's an old adage that I frequently heard adults use when I was growing up: "Do as I say, not as I do!" What a cop-out! Believe me, that didn't resonate for me and my friends when we heard it, and it's not going to fly with our children either. If we want to produce godly and morally excellent children, then they must see us live out these characteristics. The apostle Paul makes the statement to the church in Thessalonica that they should follow his Christlike example (1 Corinthians 11:1).

Many children grow up to be rebellious teens and corrupt young adults because, in large part, the things they have heard from their parents and the lives their parents have lived before them have been a contradiction between principle (what Mom said) and practice (how Mom actually lived).

Single Mothers Have a Unique Opportunity to Model Purity

Speaking of contradictions, there is no way that you can encourage your daughters to be morally pure and ask them to save themselves until God selects and sends their husband if you have a revolving door on your bedroom. Mom! No live-in "uncles"! No overnight "guests"! Sexual purity is not an easy commitment to make for most of us, I acknowledge that. However, it is one that we must be dedicated to nonetheless. As single mothers, we have an obligation to model authenticity for our daughters.

Dr. Kelly Raley, associate professor of sociology and research associate in the Population Center at the University of Texas, studies family trends and the social influences on families. In an article she cowrote in the *Sociology of Education Journal,* she presented research on single mothers that suggests that the children of mothers who have live-in boyfriends experience less success in school (Raley, Kelly, & Wildsmith 2005).

Further, the Urban Institute, a research think tank that evaluated the well-being of children living in cohabiting families, found that children six to eighteen years old exhibited increased emotional and behavioral problems, including juvenile delinquency, depression, and early involvement in premarital sex (Macomber and Moore 2009).

Not only is sexual purity important for single mothers who want to promote a genuine Christian lifestyle, it is the best choice for the social and emotional health of our daughters as well. Overall, godly parenting is the daily pursuit of living in a spirit of love and righteousness, with a forgiving heart. It is the way that we model Christ to our daughters out of a pure heart.

BASIC HOW-TOS: APPLYING
THE TACTICS THAT PRODUCE GODLY LIVING

With all of the blessings that we want to see fulfilled in our girls, the first thing to remember is that the Holy Spirit imputes righteousness! The power to change hearts belongs to God alone. He does the real grunt work. As moms, it is our responsibility to provide an atmosphere that is conducive to God being able to work in the hearts and minds of our daughters so that they will grow in righteousness.

The first tactic that we must employ is to create an environment where God can work. We must be dedicated to parenting from a biblical context. When we received Christ, it gave us a whole new approach to life and that should directly affect how we parent. Naturally, each of us has an array of old wives' tales, family traditions, speculations, and "my mom did it this way" ideas in our child-rearing toolbox. However, we must allow God's Word to supersede all of these things; it should be our primary parenting textbook. As the final authority in establishing our strategies and practices for raising our children, we give God the respect and deference that He alone deserves. In return, He gives us wisdom and insight to develop successful parenting skills.

Seasons of Life

The things I will share are, admittedly, formidable. Parenting is not for wimps. It is very time intensive. It can also be very solitary. I found it to be all of these, but it has also been the most significant, fulfilling, and important work I have ever done and, I daresay, will ever do! For the sake of your children's successful development, parenting will definitely require that you put your personal pursuits on hold. If you ever struggle with juggling your priorities, Ecclesiastes 3:1 reveals something special to hold on to: *"There is a time for everything, and a season for every activity under heaven."*

During the season of child rearing, we should budget our time based on the mandate that we covered in Deuteronomy 6:5–9 and realize that we should not "despise the day of small beginnings" (phrase borrowed from Zechariah 4:10)! Time has a way of passing quickly. My children seemed to grow up overnight. I don't have the challenges and joys of keeping five girls in line anymore. Only the laughter they left in the walls. However, I also have the freedom to revisit many of my hobbies, passions, and interests. I put down some things that were important to me in order to pursue fulfilling my purpose. My overarching goal was to dynamically disciple my daughters!

PARENTING PRECEPTS

For the mother who wants to promote godly living in her daughters, there are some very important principles that require your attention. In order to achieve your goal, you must address the following aspects of your children's lives: be purposeful, be proactive, provide protection, be prayerful, promote, praise, and reprove their behavior.

Purposeful actions. Good mothering practices require planning and preparation. I think parenting may be the job most of us come to with the least amount of forethought or training. Yet, it is the work for which we will be most remembered. The most significant legacy is not left in bricks and mortar but in the lives of the people whom we touched.

When my oldest daughter was five years old, I started to do research about home education because I thought it would give me the freedom and flexibility to implement the assignment that I take seriously from Deuteronomy 6. The organization through which I homeschooled required the families who use their curricula to write a Philosophy of Education statement. I found that to be a rather tedious undertaking.

Yet later, I realized why it was required. The formulation of my philosophy served as a mission statement and established guiding principles for me.

In fact, I referred to it frequently over the years. It proved to be an invaluable resource. It helped me prioritize activities, provided encouragement, and overall just kept me on target (which I have desperately required throughout my life, since I am very creative and can be easily distracted).

I would suggest that every family have their own mission statement to provide a similar type of benchmark. Someone once said, "If you don't know where you're going, you'll probably not wind up there." That statement came from the movie *Forrest Gump* and the character by the same name. It suggests that God really can use the simple to confound the wise!

The mission statement I devised also empowered me. There were many times when well-intentioned Christian workers, friends, and educators wanted to steer me in a different direction, or usurp my authority with the children. Single mothers are often confronted with the perception that we must have deficits in other areas because there is a lack in one, such as a lack of finances, for example.

That can be true, but it isn't always the case and those in professions that provide support need to be very careful that they do not become gratuitous, patronizing, or intrusive in their efforts to offer assistance. This behavior is not helpful and can become very undermining and damaging, making the very tenuous job of single parenting even more challenging.

Despite the challenges, I never let others dissuade or distract me—that includes the children! I had a specific road map, plans, and strategies to get me to my objective: becoming the type of woman described in Proverbs 31.

Be proactive. If our objective is to raise virtuous daughters, then we must be proactive in our approach to their development. As much as possible we want to have a specific plan of action, with goals and objectives that allow us to establish appropriate guidelines. This is especially critical to single mothers because it can help you avoid conflict with children over house rules.

For example, having specific rules about TV viewing can positively impact how your children spend their time. Do they need to invest more time in pursuing a friendship with God? Completing homework assignments? Taking care of household chores? If you don't have a clear plan in place, however, you may find that you are arguing over neglected tasks and responsibilities.

When I established guidelines in the earliest years, while the girls were toddlers, I found that maintaining discipline and standards was so much easier. Later on, as they grew older and I had to amend a house rule and increase restrictions, it was always difficult for me as I met with resistance from the girls.

Providing protection. This was one of the most important things I had to do for my girls and I took the task very seriously. I believe that children of single mothers are especially vulnerable in this area because there is a certain amount of protection and covering that comes when there is a male leader living in the house. Single women are perceived as more vulnerable, and that perception invites, to an extent, challenges to the physical, emotional, and spiritual health of those mothers and their children.

Perhaps the most significant protection a single mother can provide and the area that she has the most direct control over is the home environment that she creates. As mothers, we must guard and protect the eyes and the ears of our children. Of course, there will always be influences in the lives of our children that are beyond our control. That is all the more reason, I believe, that I had to be selective in what was seen and heard in my home.

In their book *Saving Childhood: Protecting Our Children from the National Assault on Innocence,* Michael and Diane Medved (1999) mention how childhood has been "crashed and burned" by a number of coconspirators, namely, schools, peers, the media, and so on. The negative force they refer to made the most searing impression on me; it was "the assault on innocence by parents." The Medveds caution that parents should not allow children to follow their own passions, assuming that children know what's best for them, and parents must not abdicate teaching and enforcing values and standards (1999).

We tend to hurry our children. The latest trend seems to be allowing little girls to dress and act in a very sophisticated manner. On the contrary, my girls had to beg me to stop dressing their hair with ribbons and barrettes! Once, when one of my daughters was ten years old and also 5' 7" and wearing a size 10 shoe, a friend told her that she looked like "Rebecca of Sunnybrook Farm." That was fine with me; who else should a ten-year-old look like? However, it was particularly distressing for my daughter, who begged me to forgo the two ribbons I put on the ends of her braids after that observation was made.

The Medveds (1999) go on to caution parents against not taking time to love children, rushing them through childhood, and allowing misplaced influence to affect children—like the comment made by my friend, for example. All of these instances erode our best attempts to encourage purity, chastity, and godly living.

The single biggest offender we allow in our homes, however, is the influence of television. It flies in the face of our most admirable efforts to promote morality and assaults godly Christian values. Its negative impact undermines the morals of our culture by the peer pressure it puts on society to behave in ungodly ways. The problem it creates for mothers is beyond acceptable—and we invite it in daily!

I must confess, I have unwittingly allowed behaviors into my home via television programs that I would never have let cross the threshold. Murder, assault, profane speech, vulgarity, and crass behaviors touted as "comedy" are simply debauchery! No way would I allow anyone committing such acts to come through the front door. I continue to challenge my young adult daughters that my standard is not confined to any particular age group. As such, they still hear the retort: TURN THAT THING OFF!

Be prayerful. Through personal devotions, single mothers who purpose and plan to raise daughters who love the Lord must pray without ceasing! A prudent mother sets aside a personal prayer time to gain strength and hear God's voice. We gain immeasurable benefit by focusing on our personal devotional life, and we must teach our girls how to do the same.

I cannot stress enough the importance of having a family Bible study and prayer time. Every morning we started our school day with a morning wisdom search. My girls and I read from the Bible the corresponding Proverb with that current date. We then discussed how we could apply the wisdom of it to our everyday experiences and asked God to help us in the application(s).

On Sundays, I used a prayer wheel and we prayed for one hour every Sunday evening. I chose Sunday because I wanted the entire day to be observed as God's Sabbath. Our focus was on adoration, confession, thanksgiving, supplication, time listening to God, and praise and worship time. I made a wheel with a spinner on it and the children took turns moving the spinner to the various segments on the wheel; the labels told us what to do next.

Give praise and promotion. Wise single mothers realize the power of their words and pronouncements, giving them vigorously and with gusto! Scripture supports this action: *"She openeth her mouth with wisdom; and in her tongue is the law of kindness"* (Proverbs 31:26 KJV). During Old Testament times, parents made it a consistent practice to affirm their children with a daily blessing that included a meaningful touch (a hand on their head) that expressed high value to a child. As parents visualized a special future for their offspring, they spoke life-giving words over them. We can still practice this special ritual of blessing because the effect that it brings is extremely valuable to a child's self-worth. It is a very good way to build self-esteem.

Whether knowingly, or unknowingly, we communicate to our children on a daily basis how valuable they are. They receive signals about what our expectations are and if we anticipate their success or failure. We do so by the words we say to them as well as the things they overhear us say about them. I have always taken every opportunity to "brag" on my children to friends, colleagues, and anyone who will listen when my children are present or can overhear me.

Oftentimes I have done this to their chagrin and embarrassment. My girls have chastised me numerous times for this practice. However, none of them has ever interrupted me in midspeech! I always receive these rebukes after the fact. For more on how to give a blessing to your children, refer to the book *The Blessing*, by Gary Smalley and John Trent (2004)

Reproof for correction. Finally, God's purpose for discipline is precise: *"No discipline seems pleasant at the time, but painful. Later on, however, it produces a harvest of righteousness and peace for those who have been trained by it"* (Hebrews 12:11). There are two components of biblical discipline. The first is **praise**, which includes affirmation, incentives, and rewards. Second, **reproofs** for correction must take place in the life of a child to drive foolishness from him (Proverbs 22:15 KJV). Administering correction may mean allowing a daughter to experience natural consequences for poor choices, loss of privileges, verbal reproof, and/or chastisement (for children under eight years old, in my opinion).

Of course, we should expect our daughters to obey quickly, without arguing or complaining. However, there are also circumstances when an explanation is not only warranted but necessary. When children are taught only what they should not do (don't lie) and what is appropriate (tell the truth), the result is a young woman who conforms outwardly, but does not possess the inward reality and self-control necessary to apply the overarching principle (honesty) in a variety of situations. The moral "whys" give children the information they need to become self-governing, intrinsically motivated by the Holy Spirit with knowledge about how to think and act morally and ethically.

As I have covered the various aspects of our assignment to raise godly daughters, I must address one thing that cannot be overlooked. If we do not remain accountable and faithful in the raising of our daughters, we run the risk of reaping some very negative results. No mother wants to be in this precarious position when she has to answer to God. Yet futile attempts instead of serious focus on following God's lead will not measure up.

In other words, have you ever suffered this kind of disillusionment: *"You have planted much, but have harvested little"* (Haggai 1:6)? Such was the case for the people of God during the time of the prophet Haggai. This happened to them because they did not espouse God's Word or live according to His priorities.

Just as He spoke to His people then, God speaks directly to those who are found guilty today:

> *"You expected much, but see, it turned out to be little. What you brought home, I blew away. Why?" declares the Lord Almighty. "Because of my house, which remains a ruin, while each of you is busy with his own house. Therefore, because of you the heavens have withheld their dew and the earth its crops. I called for a drought on the fields and the mountains, on the grain, the new wine, the oil and whatever the ground produces, on men and cattle, and on the labor of your hands."* (Haggai 1:9–11)

Please don't lose God's endorsement of your parenting because you value possessions and relationships, or allow any other distraction to compete for your affections. Your children deserve first place in your list of priorities.

On the flip side, I think it is important to say that despite our best efforts, children will sometimes disappoint us. They may not always make the best choices; sometimes they disobey, show disdain, ingratitude, and don't live up to our expectations. To be fair and just in our parenting, we have to consider the entire scope of the assignment. It is critical that we remain aware of this fact. I named our homeschool "Olive Tree Christian" because, like olive trees, children can live through many seasons with no fruit or noticeable growth. However, such trees live a very long time. There are some in Israel today that were there when Jesus lived on the earth! Over a period of time, the trees become fruit bearing.

Our motivation to do this tremendous and oftentimes tedious work has to be for the glory of God! We can do everything well in regard to child rearing and still not see our children follow or precisely live up to the standards we set for them as children. I have looked at each of my girls at times, then looked heavenward and posed the questions, "God! Where did this come from? What is she thinking?"

Recently, during one of these emotion-filled tirades, God responded: "Amanda, I frequently think the same thing when I look at you. Rest assured; I've got this! You look at the outward, but I look at the heart." I stood reproved and reassured.

All in all, I have a clear conscience. Despite my missteps, personal frailties, weaknesses, and sin (including the times I disciplined in error or was too lenient), I did what I knew to do, the best I knew how, with the resources available to me. I spared no expense and withheld nothing. Neither did I allow any fear to dissuade me for very long. I have a clear conscience because I have been determined to complete my assignment. I was—and will continue to be—a zealot in the lives of my daughters!

REFERENCES

Allender, D. and T. Longman. III. 1992. *Bold Love*. Colorado Springs: NavPress.

"Children's Environment and Behavior: Behavior and Emotional Problems in Children" Report publication date 1/1/09. Jennifer E. Macomber and Kristin A. Moore. Urban Institute website http://www.urban.org/publications/900870.html.

Fox, A., and B. Fox. The gift of forgiveness: giving up the emotional toxins, *Changes*, May, June, 1989, 18.

Garfinkel, I. and McLanahan, S. 1986. *Single Mothers and Their Children: A New American Dilemma* (Changing Domestic Priorities Series). Lanham, Maryland: University Press of America.

Medved, M., and D. Medved. 1999. *Saving Childhood: Protecting Our Chil-*

dren from the National Assault on Innocence. New York: Harper Paperbacks.

Raley, R., M. F. Kelly, and E. Wildsmith. 2005. Maternal cohabitation and educational success, *Sociology of Education.* Vol. 78, no. 2.

"The State of America's Children 2008 Report" second edition 12/3/08. The Children's Defense Fund website. Violence and Research Data and Publication. http://www.childrensdefense.org/child-research-data publications /data/state-of-americas-children-2008-report-moments-each-day.pdf.

Wilson, S. 1993. *Hurt People Hurt People: Hope and Healing for Yourself and Your Relationships.* Nashville: Thomas Nelson.

OUR VOICES: ISSUES FACING
BLACK WOMEN IN AMERICA

Biographies of
Contributing Writers

DR. TAFFY ANDERSON is a graduate of Georgetown University Medical School and attended the University of Michigan Hospital Department of Obstetrics and Gynecology residency program. Taffy enjoys teaching and has held academic teaching appointments at the University of Pennsylvania and Thomas Jefferson University. She has received academic awards for excellence in medical teaching from medical students and residents.

In January 2002, while serving her patients as an OB/GYN, Taffy became a patient herself; she was diagnosed with breast cancer. Her book, *Treasures in Darkness*, is the story of her journey with God and how He brought her through the storm of breast cancer, one of the darkest times of her life.

In addition to her gynecology practice, Dr. Anderson founded a company, called Healthy Living Today LLC, to promote health awareness and wellness through educational seminars and workshops. Taffy's motto is "A well-informed patient is a healthier patient." You can always be sure that she will challenge everyone to live a healthier lifestyle. To that end, Taffy tirelessly works to provide avenues for individuals to be informed about good health and wellness!

Taffy is married to the Reverend Roland H. Anderson II, who is the senior pastor of Second Baptist Church of Pottstown, Pennsylvania. As a direct result of her husband's expository preaching and knowledge-packed Bible studies, she is an avid student of the Bible and enjoys speaking to women's ministries throughout the Philadelphia area.

SABRINA D. BLACK is an author, professor, counselor, mentor, life coach, and the clinical director of Abundant Life Counseling Center, an outpatient mental health facility. Sabrina is a limited licensed professional counselor, certified addictions counselor, and certified biblical counselor with eighteen years of experience in individual, marriage, family, and group counseling. Sabrina has degrees in psychology and counseling, with expertise in the fields of gambling addiction, sexual addiction and sexual abuse, and relational problems due to substance addiction. She is also highly skilled in counseling issues relating to clergy and ministry leaders, marital conflicts and communication, boundaries and spiritual growth, stress, anxiety, burnout, and anger management.

Sabrina is a contributing author to the *Soul Care Bible,* published by Thomas Nelson; coauthor of *Prone to Wander: A Woman's Struggle with Sexual Sin and Addiction,* published by PriroityONE Publications; coeditor of *Counseling in African American Communities,* published by Zondervan; and author of *Can Two Walk Together? Encouragement for Spiritually Unbalanced Marriages,* book and Bible study guide published by Moody Publishers.

Sabrina lives in Detroit, Michigan, with her husband, Warren José Black. She has one son and four grandchildren.

VALERIE CLAYTON has a dual mission: to encourage single women to embody "wholeness" and couples to embrace "oneness." It is her desire to help women cherish their "uniqueness" and to discover their God-given gifts in order to pursue and fulfill their purpose in life. Valerie's vision is to live out God's Word to us in 2 Corinthians 1:4, *"comfort those in any trouble with the comfort we ourselves have received from God."*

Valerie and her husband, Dr. Jerome Clayton, L.C.S.W., Psy.D., have authored the book *Victory in Singleness: A Strategy for Emotional Peace.* The book addresses and provides practical solutions to the common feelings women experience when faced with prolonged singleness. *Victory in Singleness* is not a book about how to catch and keep a man. Instead, the reader is encouraged to recognize, name, and solve spiritual and emotional issues that result in poor relationship choices that lead to despair and hopelessness. *Victory in Singleness* teaches readers how to experience the peace God intends for those who are unmarried.

Valerie has over sixteen years of lay counseling experience and has encouraged hundreds of women during that period of time. The Claytons have been featured on TV and radio and have also been featured in numerous articles. They are members of Covenant Blessing Fellowship under the leadership of Pastor Donald Bell Sr. The Claytons are parents of two very, very active boys.

LISA A. CRAYTON earned her B.S. degree, *cum laude*, from Utica College of Syracuse University. She is a freelance writer, editor, conference speaker, and mentor with the Jerry B. Jenkins Christian Writers Guild. Lisa is an author of two books, including *I Want to Talk with My Teen About Money Management*. A former corporate editor and writer, Lisa spent more than five years in corporate communications for billion-dollar financial services companies. During her work with corporations, she wrote material for such diverse audiences as high-end investors, investment managers, insurance brokers, as well as benefit plan sponsors and plan participants.

As a freelancer, Lisa has written articles on financial topics for numerous regional parenting publications and other magazines. Her financial columns have appeared in *Life @ Work Journal*, *Enrichment Journal*, and *NextStep*, a magazine for high school and college students.

Lisa is very dedicated to her church where she teaches discipleship groups, leadership development classes, and a weekly women's Bible study. For several years, Lisa has been a sought-after conference workshop facilitator. She especially enjoys teaching and speaking on discipleship topics, encouraging listeners to deepen their walk with God. Lisa has one son, Josiah. Visit her online at www.LisaCrayton.com.

AMANDA JOHNSON, teacher, writer, educator, and professional model, completed her undergraduate education at the University of Kansas where she majored in human development and family life/early childhood education, and English. Later, she would go on to study at the University of Detroit-Mercy, where she earned a post B.A. paralegal certificate, receive a master's degree from the University of Michigan as a Rackham Fellow in the Center for the Study of Higher and Postsecondary Education, and matriculate at the Kellogg Foundation as a Fellow in the Evaluation Department.

Her most crowning achievement and significant life work, however, has been with her daughters, Danaeya, Serena, Allyson, Arielle, and Mariah Johnson, whom she home educated, nurtured, indulged, reproved, and loved. The girls have grown to be independent thinkers, idealistic, opinionated, articulate, accomplished, poised, and strong. In the summer of 2008, the entire family received the "Spirit of Detroit" Award from the Detroit City Council for their volunteerism.

The most important and defining relationship in Amanda's life has been the one she entered with Jesus Christ while still a young child. She responded to our Lord at the beckoning and invitation of her father, Horace Christopher. Amanda has continued to nurture and increase in her friendship with God, struggling to follow His example and to increasingly reflect Him in her standard of living.

In addition to being a voracious reader, Amanda enjoys roller-skating, swimming, ballroom dancing, decorating, shopping for fashion bargains, an array of craft and sewing projects, and of course, writing!

VICTORIA SAUNDERS JOHNSON has a bachelor's degree in counseling psychology and is currently working toward a master's degree in counseling from Trinity International University. She is a writer and speaker and has served at a number of social service agencies.

She began her service with Campus Crusade for Christ as a full-time staff member and eventually worked at Detroit's Afro-American Mission. Victoria was also involved in the Care Net of Milwaukee (a crisis pregnancy center), the Sojourner Truth House (a domestic violence agency), and New Horizon (a boys' group home). She served on the faculty at Moody Bible Institute, Milwaukee Extension, discipled many women over the years, and coordinated various women's ministry activities. A coveted workshop facilitator and conference speaker, Victoria currently serves in the women's division of the Milwaukee Rescue Mission. A native of Joliet, Illinois, Victoria currently lives in Wisconsin with her three children.

FELICIA MIDDLEBROOKS is one of the top media personalities in Chicago, Illinois, and anchors the award-winning morning drive program on CBS Radio/WBBM Newsradio 780.

Felicia is also a filmmaker. Her documentary, *Somebody's Child: The Redemption of Rwanda,* took top honors at a New York film festival in 2005.

DR. DORETHA O'QUINN has a Ph.D. in intercultural education and a master of arts degree in Christian school administration, both from Biola University. Her postgraduate studies include liberal arts education from Biola, UCLA, and Cal State Dominguez Hills, as well as a bachelor of arts degree in theology, with a minor in missions/Christian education from Life Pacific College.

Doretha is the director of the School of Education, Point Loma Nazarene University, Mission Valley Campus, San Diego, California, and an educational and business consultant, offering development, management and evaluation strategies in curriculum planning and teacher training, mentoring, organizational structure, leadership development and diversity and constructive conflict resolution training. She has served as the Associate Professor and director of the Inglewood campus of graduate studies, taught credential and teacher intern programs in education at Biola University and served as a school and business consultant, school administrator, and classroom teacher in public and Christian education institutions for over thirty years.

Doretha serves on the board of trustees of Life Pacific College and the board of directors for the International Church of the Foursquare Gospel. She has also served on multiple private and charter school boards and as an educational consultant for West Angeles Bible College Advancement and West Angeles Academy.

Doretha has published numerous articles and books, including *Women in Ministry Leadership*, published by Foursquare Publications. A member of several professional organizations, she was the recipient of the "2002 Educator of the Year Award" from West Angeles Bible College and several Los Angeles civic awards.

A coveted workshop facilitator, conference speaker, and visiting professor during the course of her forty-three-year commitment to the Lord, Doretha has traveled extensively to Panama, Central America; the cities of Calexico and Ensenada, Mexico; London; Germany; Martinique Island, Puerto Rico; Israel; East, West, and South Africa.

Doretha has been married to Michael O'Quinn for thirty-five years. The couple has four children and three grandchildren.

YOLANDA L. POWELL is a graduate of Clark-Atlanta University. She is the ministry director of Oracles & Utterance, Inc., a Christian communications ministry based in southern Maryland. Yolanda is committed to "Transforming Lives by the Spoken Word!" Her dedication as a Bible student fuels her innovative Bible teaching and creative approach to imparting the timeless truths of God's Word.

Yolanda is also a fiery evangelist who has led many to the saving knowledge of Jesus Christ and has ministered throughout the country at churches, women's retreats, youth events, and convocations. She and her husband were recently chosen as Small Church Instructors with "Walk Thru the Bible Ministries." They will lead an Urban Walk of Old Testament Seminars throughout the DC/Maryland/Virginia area and conduct workshops for Christian schools in the Mid-Atlantic region. Yolanda and William reside in Huntingtown, Maryland, with their three sons.

KAREN WADDLES is a contributing author for the *Women of Color Devotional Bible* (Nia Publishing) and the *Teen Devotional* (Nia Publishing). She has a degree in counseling from DePaul University and is employed by Moody Publishers.

Karen is a member of the Zion Hill Baptist Church where her husband serves as pastor. She is an instructor in the National Baptist Congress of Christian Education and a women's conference speaker. Karen and her husband are the proud parents of four adult children and eight grandchildren.

ACKNOWLEDGMENTS

My most sincere thanks to Karen at Moody. Thank you for giving me and my coauthors a voice.

Thank you to Yulon, David M., Pat B., Larry R., Betty C., Renee G., Anita R., Christy H., Clifton W., Dian C., Joyce G., and Deena D. for your consistent love, prayers, encouragements, support, and friendship.

Jo Ann and Mrs. Lloyd, for your hospitality and generosity when all I could offer was a thank-you.

Finally, for your unwavering support, friendship, investments of countless hours in counseling, and every type of resource, including housing, meals, companionship, music lessons, math tutoring, child care, lawn mowers, transportation, and untold gifts of financial support and service—all the acts of love that are usually confined to families . . . For sharing your lives with the children and me and making every conceivable sacrifice to ensure our success, individually and collectively. It is true that God sets the lonely in families because Lydia, Terry and Janice, and Mike you have been that for me, but most especially, Renee Allyson.

"May the Lord repay you for what you have done. May you be richly rewarded of the Lord, the God of Israel, under whose wings you have come to take refuge." Ruth 2:12

TREASURES IN DARKNESS

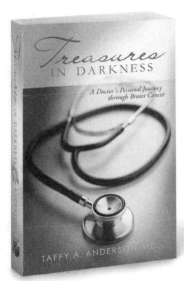

In this inspiring, true story, Dr. Taffy Anderson illuminates the treasures of darkness she gathered while fighting–and surviving– breast cancer. Both a medical and spiritual journal of her experience, *Treasures in Darkness* traces her journey from a busy OB/GYN at a major medical hospital who learns of her older sister's diagnosis with breast cancer, to her own shocking diagnosis three years later, through painful surgery, chemo treatments, and coming face-to-face with death. Along the way, she learns to submit to the sovereign will of God, draw strength from His presence and cherish each day of life.

www.lifteveryvoicebooks.com

1-800-678-8812 • MOODYPUBLISHERS.COM

VICTORY IN SINGLENESS

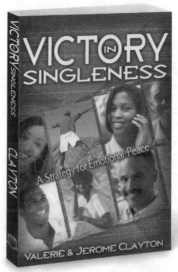

ISBN-13: 978-0-8024-4015-0

An astounding sixty-two percent of African-American women are single! Often these women are saddled with envy, discouragement, and bitterness. Valerie and Jerome Clayton have written *Victory in Singleness* to help African-American singles find viable solutions to their real-life hurt so they can become all God has called them to be. Readers will find hope and learn how to develop a strategy for emotional peace by ridding themselves of the baggage weighing them down.

www.lifteveryvoicebooks.com
1-800-678-8812 • MOODYPUBLISHERS.COM

SEVEN REASONS WHY GOD CREATED MARRIAGE

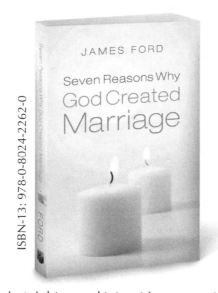

ISBN-13: 978-0-8024-2262-0

Marriage is a wonderful thing and it is without question a part of God's plan for many. So what is this thing called marriage and what are some of the foundational things you need to know as you anticipate growing old with your mate? In *Seven Reasons Why God Created Marriage*, Pastor James Ford, a seasoned marriage counselor, walks readers through the Bible and shows them seven purposes for which God created marriage. This exploration will reveal timeless truths upon which readers—whether engaged of newly married—can build a solid foundation and strengthen the pillars of their marriage, reaping the benefits God intended along the way.

L E V B
LIFT EVERY VOICE BOOKS

www.lifteveryvoicebooks.com

1-800-678-8812 • ·MOODYPUBLISHERS.COM

CAN TWO WALK TOGETHER?

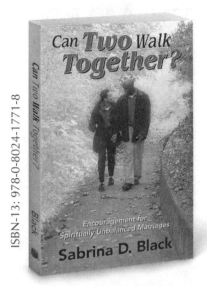

Find spiritual balance in your marriage. Many Christians are in
spiritually unbalanced marriages, desperate for someone to minister to them in their unique place. This is a wonderful tool to
provide those in unequally yoked relationships with hope and
help in dealing with disappointment, hurts, and heartaches. Sabrina Black brings her counseling expertise to bear on this difficult subject, assisting couples with creating and maintaining a
vibrant, growing relationship despite their differences.

www.lifteveryvoicebooks.com
1-800-678-8812 • MOODYPUBLISHERS.COM

LEE JENKINS ON MONEY

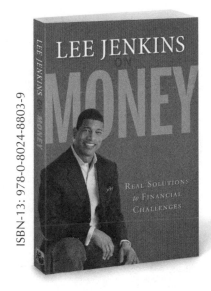

ISBN-13: 978-0-8024-8803-9

In *Lee Jenkins on Money*, financial analyst Lee Jenkins answers questions about the nation's changing economy and other financial matters that readers may be facing in the midst of this difficult financial climate. He helps them take a sober and responsible look at their finances and challenges them to be faithful stewards over what God has entrusted to them. Lee shows that by looking at life from God's perspective and applying biblical principles to their finances, readers bear witness to the fact that God is still in control and there is still hope.

LEVB
LIFT EVERY VOICE BOOKS
www.lifteveryvoicebooks.com
1-800-678-8812 • MOODYPUBLISHERS.COM

THE TRAUMA ZONE

ISBN-13: 978-0-8024-8989-0

Some cannot move forward, feeling stuck and victimized by their past. Some cannot see the present, living in denial of what has happened. And others cannot learn from the past, repeating the same mistakes over and over. All of them find they can't cope with the overwhelming emotions that accompany trauma. Collins, a licensed psychologist with over 25 years experience in the healthcare field, believes there is a way out of the trauma zone and back to emotional health, a path he outlines in this practical, encouraging book.

www.lifteveryvoicebooks.com
1-800-678-8812   •   MOODYPUBLISHERS.COM

Lift Every Voice Books

Lift every voice and sing
Till earth and heaven ring,
Ring with the harmonies of Liberty;
Let our rejoicing rise
High as the listening skies,
Let it resound loud as the rolling sea.
Sing a song full of the faith that the dark past has taught us,
Sing a song full of the hope that the present has brought us,
Facing the rising sun of our new day begun
Let us march on till victory is won.

The Black National Anthem, written by James Weldon Johnson in 1900, captures the essence of Lift Every Voice Books. Lift Every Voice Books is an imprint of Moody Publishers that celebrates a rich culture and great heritage of faith, based on the foundation of eternal truth—God's Word. We endeavor to restore the fabric of the African-American soul and reclaim the indomitable spirit that kept our forefathers true to God in spite of insurmountable odds.

We are Lift Every Voice Books—Christ-centered books and resources for restoring the African-American soul.

For more information on other books and products
written and produced from a biblical perspective,
go to www.lifteveryvoicebooks.com or write to:

Lift Every Voice Books
820 N. LaSalle Boulevard
Chicago, IL 60610
www.lifteveryvoicebooks.com